Egermeier's
PICTURE-STORY
LIFE OF JESUS

by

Elsie E. Egermeier

Story Revisions
by Arlene S. Hall

Adapted from Egermeier's Bible Story Book

Warner Press
Anderson, Indiana

Lithographed in the United States of America

A WORD TO BEGIN

Towering above all the characters whom the world calls great stands one Person—Jesus Christ. Everybody should know about him.

Adults find the record of his marvelous life in the Book of books. There, in language familiar to them, they read all about him, and they conclude that he was the greatest, the kindest, and the most helpful Person this world has ever known.

Children, too, should be given the opportunity to read about him. And so, because picture-language is more familiar to children, and story-language is more easily understood by them, we present here in pictures and stories a record of the Life of Christ.

—Elsie E. Egermeier

The Stories in This Book

A Wonderful Baby's Birth

Luke 2:1-39

The people of Nazareth were excited! The Roman emperor had commanded everyone to enroll in the town or city from which his family had come. No one dared disobey his command.

Soon travelers were going in every direction. Joseph and Mary were going to Bethlehem, for they were both of the family of David.

From Nazareth a company of people started toward the south. The road led through Samar'ia and over the Judean hills to Jerusalem. From Jerusalem Joseph and Mary went farther south until they came to Bethlehem. Some of their company left them in cities along the way, while other people joined them.

When they reached Bethlehem, it was crowded with people. No place could be found for new arrivals. The journey from Nazareth had been long and hard. How much Mary wanted a place to rest! Joseph could find only the stable of the inn. That night Baby Jesus was born. Mary wrapped him in soft cloths called swaddling clothes and laid him in a manger.

Shepherds were watching their flocks that night near Bethlehem.

Suddenly the angel of the Lord came near, and a great light shone through the darkness. The shepherds were afraid. Why had the angel come to them?

The angel said, "Fear not, for I bring you good tidings of great joy, which shall be to all people. For unto you is born this day in the city of David a Savior, which is Christ the Lord. And you shall find the baby wrapped in swaddling clothes, lying in a manger."

What wonderful news! Many angels sang, "Glory to God in the highest, and on earth peace, good will toward men." Then the angels returned to heaven, and the light faded into the still darkness of the night.

The shepherds said to each other, "Let us now go to Bethlehem and see this thing which the Lord has made known to us."

Leaving their flocks, they hurried to Bethlehem. There in a stable they found Mary and Joseph and the infant Savior. Kneeling before the manger, they worshiped the little babe who lay quietly sleeping on the hay.

They told Mary and Joseph, "An angel of the Lord told us the news and an angelic choir sang praise to God." On the way back to their flocks they told everyone they met about the angel's visit and the Savior's birth.

When the baby was eight days old, Joseph and Mary named him Jesus, the name the angel had chosen. The name Jesus means salvation.

According to Jewish law each family had to make an offering to the Lord for their first baby boy. Rich people gave a lamb; poor people, two young pigeons. When Jesus was forty days old, Joseph and Mary took him to the temple at Jerusalem. They offered two young pigeons to the Lord, for they were poor.

Old Simeon was in the temple. God had promised him, "You shall not die until you have seen the Savior." When Mary brought Baby Jesus to the temple, God's Spirit made Simeon know that this child was the promised Savior.

Simeon came eagerly to meet Mary and took the baby in his arms. "Now may God let me depart in peace, for I have seen with my eyes the salvation which he has sent," Simeon said.

Joseph and Mary
called the baby Jesus.

Anna was an old woman who had served God faithfully all her life. When she saw Jesus, she too gave thanks to God.

Mary never forgot what Simeon and Anna said about Jesus, nor did she forget the story the shepherds told. She thought about these strange things and wondered how her son Jesus would finally become the Savior of the world.

The Wise Men Follow a Star

Matthew 2

Far to the east of Judea lived certain Wise Men who studied the stars. One night they discovered a new star. By this God made them know that Christ had been born.

These Wise Men feared God, and they wanted to see the child who was to be the Savior of the world. At once they planned to take rich gifts to the newborn king and to worship him as their Savior.

Many days they traveled across the desert to Judea. They hurried to Jerusalem, for surely the wonderful child would be in the most beautiful and famous city.

Herod, the ruler, was troubled. Why were these strangers riding on camels into his city? Why did they ask, "Where is he that is born king of the Jews? We have seen his star in the east and have come to worship him."

Herod knew nothing about the newborn king. What can this mean? he wondered. Calling the chief priests and scribes, he demanded, "Where is the Savior to be born?"

The chief priests and scribes remembered what the prophets had written long ago. They answered, "The Savior is to be born in Bethlehem. He is to rule his people."

Now Herod was more worried. What if this newborn king should take away his throne? Secretly he called the Wise Men and asked, "When did you see this star?" When they told him, he said, "Go to Bethlehem and search diligently for the young child. When you have found him, let me know that I may come and worship him."

Outside the city gates the Wise Men saw the same bright star they had seen in the east country. It seemed to lead them. Surely God was helping them find Jesus.

At Bethlehem the star stood still over the place where Jesus was. At last they had found the newborn king! Falling to their knees they worshiped him. Opening their treasures, they gave him rich gifts—gold, frankincense, and myrrh.

Before the Wise Men left Bethlehem, God told them in a dream not to go back to Herod. So they returned to their own country by another road.

Not long afterwards an angel of the Lord said to Joseph in a dream, "Arise, and take the young child and his mother, and flee to Egypt. Stay there until I tell you to return, for Herod will look for Jesus and try to kill him." Joseph got up, took Mary and Baby Jesus, and hurried out of Bethlehem. They traveled until they came to the country of Egypt.

Herod waited a long time for the Wise Men to return from Bethlehem, but they never came. Maybe they had guessed why he had been so eager to see Jesus. Now Herod was angry! He had not found the newborn king!

Herod sent his soldiers to kill every child two years old or less in Bethlehem and the country round about. Surely this would get rid of Jesus!

But Jesus was safe in Egypt. When Herod died, an angel told Joseph, "Arise, take the young child and his mother and go back."

Back to Bethlehem they started. In Judea Joseph learned that Herod's son was now ruler. What if the new king were like his father? Because Joseph was afraid, they went on to Nazareth. Here they made their home, and Joseph opened his carpenter's shop.

When Jesus Was a Boy

Luke 2:40-52

As a little boy, Jesus loved to watch Joseph work and to play with the shavings that fell from his bench. Of course Jesus liked to run and play outdoors with his friends too.

Nazareth, Jesus' home town, was nearly seventy miles from Jeru-

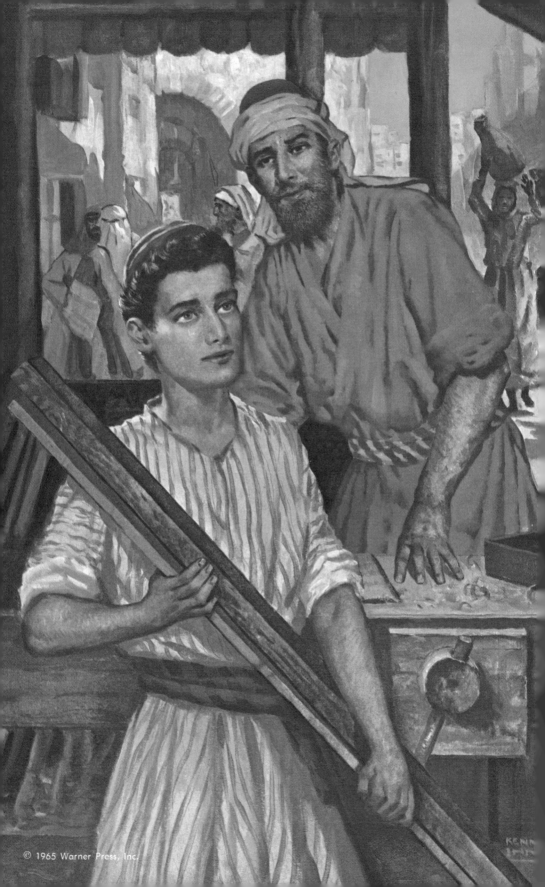

salem. The people could not go every week to worship God at the temple in Jerusalem. Instead they built a synagogue in Nazareth. Here they heard the reading of books written by Moses and the prophets.

When Jesus was old enough to go to school, Mary and Joseph sent him to the synagogue. It was here Jewish boys learned to read and write. They studied the psalms and the writings of Moses and the prophets. Like other Jewish boys, Jesus learned many Scripture verses by memory, for no one had a Bible of his own.

One spring morning a company of Jews left Nazareth for the Feast of the Passover at Jerusalem. Joseph and Mary had gone to this feast every year since their return from Egypt. But the feast would be different for them this year. They were taking Jesus for the first time. Now that Jesus was twelve, he would be going every year.

As the company moved slowly down the road, people from other cities and villages joined them. At Jerusalem they met people from every part of the land. What an exciting time this was! How wide Jesus' eyes must have been when he saw the beautiful temple!

Jesus began to understand that God was his Father and that he must work with God. Each day at the temple he listened to the chief priests and scribes and asked them questions.

After the feast the people from Nazareth started home. Mary did not see Jesus, but she thought he was with their friends and relatives.

Evening came and still Mary did not see Jesus. Joseph and she began to search for him. All through the company they asked, "Have you seen Jesus?" Always the answer was the same. No one had seen him that day.

Now Mary and Joseph were very worried. They turned back to Jerusalem, hunting for Jesus.

On the third day they found him. He was not playing with other boys in the streets or learning to swim in the Pool of Siloam. Jesus was at the temple with the wise teachers, listening to them and asking questions.

How surprised Mary was to find Jesus there! She said, "Son, why did you stay here when we were starting for home? Your father and I have been so worried! We've looked everywhere for you."

13

Jesus learns to
be a carpenter.

Jesus answered, "Why did you look for me? Didn't you know that I would be at my Father's house?"

Mary did not understand. What did Jesus mean?

Jesus had surprised the teachers in the temple. He asked questions they could not answer.

As the years passed Jesus grew to be a noble young man. He learned to explain the Scriptures and to talk with God. By helping Joseph with his work, Jesus also became a carpenter. When Joseph died, Jesus worked to care for Mary and for his brothers and sisters. His kind, thoughtful ways won him many friends. Jesus lived in his Nazareth home until he was about thirty years old.

John Preaches in the Wilderness

Matthew 3:1-12; Mark 1:3-8; Luke 3:1-20; John 1:15-28

When John was about thirty years old, he left his home and went throughout the hill country of Judea. He preached, "Repent, for the kingdom of heaven is at hand." Instead of going to the cities to preach God's message, John stayed in the country near the river Jordan.

People came from every part of the land to hear him speak. For more than four hundred years no great prophet had arisen to speak God's words to the people. No wonder they were eager to hear John!

When the people gathered to hear this strange desert preacher, they saw a man dressed in rough clothing made of camel's hair. About his waist was a leather girdle. Because he spent all his time preaching in the country, his food was dried locusts and wild honey.

Many who heard John's preaching repented of their sins. Some found fault, but all were impressed. News of this strange preacher spread to the farthest corners of the land. Everywhere people wondered, "Who is this man?"

The Jews at Jerusalem sent priests and Levites to ask John, "Who are you?"

John said, "I am not the Christ."

"Are you Elijah?" they asked. When John said he was not, they wanted to know, "Are you a prophet?" Again John's answer was no. Finally the priests and Levites asked, "Then who are you? Tell us so we will know what to report to the people who sent us."

To this John said, "I am the voice of one crying in the wilderness, 'Make straight the way of the Lord.' "

Still the priests and Levites had another question. "Why do you baptize people if you are not Christ, or Elijah, or a prophet?"

"I baptize with water," John explained. "There is a great one coming whose shoes I am not worthy to unloose. He will baptize you with the Holy Spirit."

In the crowds to whom John preached were all kinds of people. Usually there were a few Pharisees and Sadducees, the religious rulers of the Jews. They seemed to be very religious, but in their hearts many of them were proud and sinful. They thought they were more righteous than other people.

One time some Pharisees and Sadducees came to John to be baptized. He said to them, "Who has warned you evil men to flee from God's anger? You will not be ready to enter God's kingdom."

Those who believed John's preaching and repented of their sins asked him, "What should we do now?"

He answered, "The person who has two coats should give one to the man who has none. He who has more food than he needs should share with those who are hungry."

The tax collectors listened closely. Then they wanted to know what they should do. John told them, "Do not ask for more tax money than you are supposed to."

Soldiers, too, wondered what they should do now that they had repented of their sins. "Do not hurt or falsely accuse any man. Be content with your wages."

In the Jordan River John baptized those who confessed their sins. For that reason the people called him "John the Baptist."

John Baptizes Jesus

Matthew 3:13-17; Mark 1:9-11; Luke 3:21-22; John 1:29-34

Jesus was thirty years old when he left Nazareth and went to the Jordan River where John preached and baptized the people. When John saw Jesus in the crowd he called out, "This is the Lamb of God that takes away the sin of the world. This is the one who is greater than I."

But Jesus had not come to be introduced to the people; he wanted to be baptized. John said, "Why have you come to be baptized? You are much greater than I." John felt unworthy to baptize the Son of God.

Jesus answered, "I must be baptized because it is God's plan. Baptize me now." And John took Jesus into the river and baptized him there.

When the two were coming out of the water, a strange thing happened. The heavens opened and the Spirit of God in the form of a dove came down upon Jesus. A voice from heaven said, "This is my beloved Son in whom I am well pleased."

Jesus Is Tempted

Matthew 4:1-11; Mark 1:12-13; Luke 4:1-14

After Jesus' baptism, he was led by the Spirit of God into the wilderness. Jesus knew the great work God wanted him to do. Now he spent many days thinking and praying about it.

After forty days in the wilderness, the tempter came to Jesus. Because he knew Jesus was weak and hungry, he said, "If you are the Son of God, command that these stones become loaves of bread."

Even though Jesus was very hungry, he refused. He would not use God's great power just to please himself. Instead he trusted his heavenly Father to care for his needs. To the tempter he said, "It is written, 'Man shall not live by bread alone, but by every word of God.'"

When this temptation failed, the devil tried another. Taking Jesus to the roof of the temple he said, "If you expect people to believe

16

John baptizes
Jesus in the river.

that you are really God's Son, you must show some great signs. Now jump off and trust God to protect you from getting hurt. In the Scripture he has promised that his angels will not let any harm come to you."

Satan tempted Jesus with an easy way to get followers. Even though Satan had used words of Scripture, Jesus did not do this foolish thing. He knew the Scriptures forbid a person to do anything foolish and then expect God's angels to help him. He reminded the devil, "It is said, 'Thou shalt not tempt the Lord thy God.' "

Finally on a high mountain the devil showed Jesus all the kingdoms of the world. "These great kingdoms are mine," the tempter said, "and I can give them to anyone I choose. I will give them to you if you will fall down and worship me."

Jesus did not weaken. He answered, "Get away from me, you evil one! For it is written, 'Thou shalt worship the Lord thy God, and him only shalt thou serve.' "

At last Satan left Jesus alone, and angels came from heaven to care for Jesus' needs. He had won a great victory over the devil. Now he was ready to do his Father's work.

Jesus Makes Five New Friends

John 1:35-51

Many people believed the message John preached. With new eagerness they awaited the coming of the King from heaven. How glad they would be to hear that their King had arrived! In their hearts they believed he would set up a kingdom like David's, and the Jews would be his favored people.

One day John the Baptist saw Jesus walking along the road near the river. John cried out, "Behold the Lamb of God!"

Two of John's disciples had heard John say so many wonderful things about Jesus that they turned and followed him. When Jesus saw the two men coming after him, he asked, "What do you want?"

They answered, "Master, where do you live?"

"Come and see," Jesus said. Jesus took the two with him and they talked all day.

Never had they heard a man speak as Jesus did! Andrew, one of the two, got so excited about what he heard that he ran to find his brother Simon. Simon, too, must hear. Both Andrew and Simon believed that John the Baptist was a prophet of God. They listened to him often and followed him wherever he went.

Already Andrew was sure that he had found a teacher even greater than John. When Andrew found Simon, he called out, "Come with me, for we have found the Messiah!" And the two hurried back to Jesus.

When Jesus saw the brothers, he looked at Simon and said, "You are Simon, the son of Jona; but you shall be called Peter."

How surprised Simon was! How did Jesus know his name? Jesus seemed to know all about him. As Simon listened, he too believed that Jesus was the Christ. Now he was just as eager to follow Jesus as Andrew was.

The next day Jesus started back to his home in Galilee. With him were his three new friends. As they walked along, they met a man named Philip. He lived in the same town as Simon and Andrew.

To Philip Jesus said, "Follow me." And Philip did.

As Philip walked with Jesus and the other three he marveled at the wise words Jesus spoke. Surely this was the promised Savior and king. Philip was so thrilled that he ran to find his friend Nathan'ael. Philip told him, "We have found the one Moses and the prophets wrote about, Jesus of Nazareth."

Because Nathanael knew the Scriptures well, he remembered that the prophet had written that the king of the Jews would be born in Bethlehem. So he asked Philip, "Can any good thing come from Nazareth?"

Philip did not waste a minute trying to convince his friend. Instead he said, "Come and see."

Because Philip was so eager, Nathanael went along. When Jesus saw Nathanael, he said, "Look, an Israelite in whom there is no deceit!"

Nathanael was astonished. "How do you know me?" he asked.

"Before Philip called you," Jesus said, "I saw you under the fig tree."

How could Jesus have known where he was and what he was doing?

19

At once Nathanael believed that Jesus came from God. With joy he exclaimed, "Master, you are the Son of God! You are the King of Israel!"

Jesus said, "Do you believe just because I said I saw you under the fig tree? You shall see greater things than these."

The Wedding at Cana

John 2:1-11

A family in Cana of Galilee gave a feast. One of the family was to be married, and they had invited many people to the wedding. Among the guests were Jesus, his mother, and his followers.

The wedding feast lasted several days. Perhaps these people were poor, or maybe they had not expected so many friends to come. The feast was not over, but the wine was all gone.

When Jesus' mother found out about this, she called her son aside. "They have no more wine," she explained. Wouldn't he help their friends at a time like this?

Mary called the servants. Pointing to Jesus, she said, "Do whatever he tells you."

And Jesus told them, "Fill the water pots with water."

And the servants filled the huge jars to the brim. Then Jesus said, "Pour out some and take it to the governor of the feast."

Again they obeyed. But instead of water, wine came out of the great stone jars. How surprised they were! Quickly they carried some to the governor of the feast, for he had to taste everything before it was served to the guests.

The governor took the wine without knowing what had happened. When he tasted it, he was surprised that this was much better than the wine that had already been served.

At once the governor called the bridegroom and told him, "At other .wedding feasts the best wine is served first, but you have kept the best until the last."

This was Jesus' first miracle. By it he had helped people who were in need. The men who were with Jesus marveled at what he had done. Surely no man could do such miracles!

Jesus Keeps the Passover

John 2:13-25

At the time of the Passover, people from every part of the land went up to Jerusalem to keep the feast. Among those who went were Jesus and his friends—Andrew, Simon, Philip, and Nathanael.

When Jesus entered the temple court, he found it crowded, noisy, and busy. Nothing about it made a person feel like praying. It looked more like a market than a house of prayer. Men had brought live oxen, sheep, and doves into the temple to sell for sacrifices. These animals only added to the noise and confusion.

In one corner money-changers sat at small tables. Every Jew over twenty years old had to give a piece of silver money called a half shekel to the priests. This money was used for sacrifices and for the temple.

Those who came from distant countries brought the kind of money used in their homeland. Since half shekels were the only coins the priests would take, all other coins had to be changed for half shekels to pay the priests. Every person had to pay to have his money changed into temple coins.

How angry Jesus was when he saw people making a market place out of God's house! Taking small cords, he tied them together and made a whip. With the whip he drove out all the animals and their keepers. Then he upset the money-changers' tables. To those who sold doves he said, "Take these things away. Do not make my Father's house a house of selling."

Many Jews were angry at Jesus for doing this. They asked, "What sign do you show that you have a right to do such things?"

Jesus knew they would not believe him even if he showed them a sign. He answered, "Destroy this temple, and in three days I will raise it up." Jesus meant the temple of his body. He knew the Jews would help to kill him. Then in three days he would rise from the dead.

The Jews did not understand. They thought Jesus meant the great temple Herod had rebuilt on Mount Moriah. They scoffed, "It took forty-six years to build this temple, and you say you can rebuild it in three days!" Shaking their heads doubtfully they walked away.

During the feast Jesus began to teach the people and to do miracles among them. Many believed in him when they heard his words and saw the great works that no other man could do.

Nicodemus Comes to Jesus

John 3:1-21

One man who believed in Jesus was a ruler among the Jews. He was Nicode'mus, a rich Pharisee. Most of the Pharisees were very proud. They did not believe that either John the Baptist or Jesus were teachers sent from God.

Nicodemus was not like the other Pharisees. He heard Jesus teach the people who had come to worship at the Passover. "Surely Jesus is very great," Nicodemus thought.

While other Pharisees were finding fault with Jesus, Nicodemus wanted to hear more of his teachings. One night he went to the place where Jesus stayed to talk with him.

Nicodemus said, "Master, we know you are a teacher from God. No man could do the miracles you do unless God was with him."

Jesus wanted Nicodemus to know about the kingdom of God. He said, "Unless a man is born again, he cannot see the kingdom of God."

Nicodemus was puzzled. He asked, "How can a man be born after he is grown up? Can he become a tiny baby again?"

Jesus did not mean that a man would be born again in body but in heart. He said, "Unless a man is born of water and of the Spirit, he cannot enter the kingdom of God. Do not be surprised when I say that you must be born again. The wind blows. You hear it and you see what it does. Yet you do not see the wind itself. You cannot tell where it comes from or where it goes. That is the way it is with those who are born again."

Nicodemus thought about Jesus' words. No one could see the Spirit. Yet a person whose heart was changed, born again, would act as if he had the Spirit of God in his heart.

Finally Jesus said tenderly, "God so loved the world that he gave his only begotten Son, that whosoever believeth in him should not perish, but have everlasting life."

The Woman at the Well

John 4:1-43

Jesus decided to return to Galilee. He and his disciples took the shorter road that led through Samar'ia. Not many Jews went this way because they hated the Samar'itans. Although both the Jews and the Samaritans worshiped God, the Samaritans had built a temple in their own country instead of going to Jerusalem to worship.

In many ways Jesus was not like most other Jews. For one thing he did not feel bitter towards the Samaritans. He knew that God loved the people of every land.

When they had traveled as far as the little city of Sychar, Jesus was tired. He sat down to rest by a well Jacob had dug hundreds of years before. Here his disciples left him and went into the city to buy food.

Soon a woman from Sychar came to get water. She knew at a glance that the strange man sitting there was a Jew. Since Jews paid no attention to Samaritans, she passed by him and lowered her water jar into the deep well. When the water jar was full, she pulled it up again.

Just as the woman was ready to start back to the city, Jesus said, "Give me a drink."

The woman was so surprised at his request that she said, "Since you are a Jew, why do you ask a Samaritan woman for a drink? You know the Jews have nothing to do with the Samaritans."

Jesus replied, "If you knew who asks you for a drink, you would ask him to give you living water."

The woman did not understand. She said, "Sir, this well is deep and you have nothing to draw the water up with. How could you give me living water? Are you greater than Jacob who gave us this well?"

"Whoever drinks of this water becomes thirsty and returns again and again for more," Jesus answered. "Whoever drinks the water that I give will never be thirsty again. The water that I give springs up into everlasting life."

Now the woman was really interested. She did not know that the living water was Jesus' free gift of salvation to all people. So she

said, "Sir, give me this water so I won't have to come here to get water any more."

And Jesus told the woman things about herself that she thought no one knew. He told her about the wrongs she had done.

The woman wondered how this stranger could know all about her. Then she decided, "Sir, I believe you are a prophet." Because she did not want to be reminded of her sins, she tried to start an argument about religion. She said, "We Samaritans worship here, but you Jews say people should go to Jerusalem to worship."

Jesus did not argue. Instead he explained that God planned to bring salvation through the Jews. "God is not found in only one place," he said, "for God is Spirit. Those who worship him must worship in spirit and in truth."

The woman had never heard such wonderful words. She said, "I know the Messiah, the Christ, is coming from God. When he comes, he will tell us everything."

How surprised the woman was when she heard Jesus say, "I am he"! Before she could ask him more, the disciples returned with food. Leaving her water jar by the well, she ran to tell her friends about this wonderful stranger.

When the disciples saw Jesus talking with the Samaritan woman, they wished they dared ask him, "What do you want? Why do you talk with her?" Instead they offered him food. "Master, eat," they said.

Jesus refused. He said, "I have food to eat that you know nothing about."

And the disciples whispered to one another, "Did someone bring him food while we were away?"

Jesus knew their question so he said, "My food is to do the will of my Father who has sent me into the world."

Back in the city the woman ran through the streets telling the people about Jesus. "Come see a man who told me all the things I ever did," she said. "Is not he the Christ?"

The people were so curious that they decided to see this man for themselves. They went back to Jacob's well with her.

Jesus talked with the Samaritans about the things of God. They invited him to stay and teach them more, and Jesus agreed.

25

**Jesus explains how
God plans to bring salvation.**

For two days Jesus taught the people of Sychar. Many believed. They said to the woman who first met Jesus at the well, "Now we believe. Not because of what you told us, but because we heard for ourselves, we know this man is the Christ, the Savior of the world."

Jesus took his disciples and went on to Nazareth.

Jesus Heals the Nobleman's Son

John 4:45-54

Many people of Galilee were eager to see Jesus. It was told throughout the country that Jesus had turned the water to wine at Cana. Since then word had come about his teachings and his miracles in Jerusalem during the Passover. When Jesus entered Galilee from Samar'ia news of his coming spread rapidly from one city to another. Everywhere people hoped Jesus would come to their cities and work miracles.

One man could not wait for Jesus to come to his city. He went looking for Jesus. He was a nobleman, an honored ruler of the city of Caper'naum. How worried he was because his little son lay sick with a burning fever! The doctors could not help the little boy. How much the father wanted to see his son well again!

As soon as the nobleman heard about Jesus, he hurried to find him. When he found Jesus, he pleaded with the Master to come and heal his son. Without Jesus' healing touch, the child might die.

So many people were following Jesus just to see him work miracles that Jesus said, "Unless you see signs and wonders you will not believe that I am sent of God."

Again the nobleman begged, "Sir, if you do not come at once, my son may be dead before we reach him."

Jesus looked kindly at the distressed father. He said, "Go back home. Your son lives."

Because the nobleman believed Jesus' words, he started back to Capernaum. No longer was he afraid for his son. Jesus had said the boy was well.

As the nobleman approached Capernaum, his servants came running to meet him. He could tell by their faces that they had good news. "Your son lives. He is well," they said.

"At what time," asked the nobleman, "did he begin to get better?"

And the servants replied, "His fever left him yesterday at the seventh hour."

That was the very hour Jesus had told the nobleman, "Your son lives." Not only the nobleman but also all his household believed in Jesus when they heard how the sick boy had been healed.

Jesus Speaks at Nazareth

Luke 4:16-32

"Jesus is home." "Jesus is back in Nazareth." The news spread quickly from one person to another.

The people of Nazareth had heard about Jesus' teachings and miracles in other cities. Now they wanted to hear for themselves what Joseph's son would say. Jesus stood up in the synagogue to read, and the leader brought him the book the prophet Isaiah had written long years before. Jesus read these words about the promised Savior:

"The Spirit of the Lord is upon me,
Because he has anointed me to preach the gospel to the poor;
He has sent me to heal the brokenhearted,
To preach deliverance to the captives,
And recovering of sight to the blind,
To set at liberty them that are bruised,
To preach the acceptable year of the Lord."

After reading these words, Jesus closed the book, gave it back to the leader and sat down. The speaker in the synagogue always stood up to read God's words and sat down to explain their meaning.

Among those who listened were people who had known Jesus nearly all his life. Proud men they were, unwilling to learn new truths. They had heard of Jesus' miracles in Cana and Caper'naum, but they

27

did not believe he was the promised Savior. Jesus was only a poor man. They expected the Savior to be rich and powerful.

Everyone watched and waited for Jesus to speak. How surprised they were when they heard his words! They did not know he could speak so well. Little did they know that Jesus was the world's greatest teacher.

His words pleased them until he said, "Today Isaiah's words have come true. I am the one who is to preach the gospel to the poor and the captives, to heal and to help as Isaiah promised."

"How could this be true?" they asked each other. "Is not this Joseph's son?"

Jesus knew they would not believe him. No prophet is honored by his own people. Jesus said, "One time Elijah the prophet ran away from Israel to hide in the home of a poor widow in a heathen land. Because this poor widow cared for God's prophet, God took care of her. God healed Na'aman, the heathen leper, when he obeyed Eli'sha's words. Yet many Israelites had leprosy and never were healed."

The proud men of Nazareth were angry. Was Jesus telling them that God cared for other people besides the Jews? They would not listen to such words! The leading men ran to Jesus, grabbed him, and pulled him outside the synagogue. An angry mob followed.

The mob led Jesus to the top of the high hill on which Nazareth was built. They planned to throw him over the edge upon the sharp rocks far below. Strangely enough Jesus walked quietly through the excited mob, and they did not see him go.

Jesus went to Capernaum, the city by the Sea of Galilee. Here he taught the people about God, and the people were glad to listen.

Many Fish

Luke 5:1-11

After some time Jesus returned to Capernaum to teach the people, and his disciples went back to their work as fishermen. One day Jesus walked to the seashore where Simon Peter, Andrew, James, and John were washing their nets.

29

Jesus reads Isaiah's words
in the synagogue.

Many people had seen Jesus leave the city, and they followed. Soon a great crowd gathered on the shore. How eager they were to hear Jesus preach!

Jesus stepped into Peter's boat and moved it just out from shore.

There Jesus spoke to the people. After teaching them, he told Simon, "Move out into the deep and let down your nets for a catch."

Simon replied, "Master, we have fished all night, and we have caught nothing." Then he added, "But if you say so, we will try again."

Simon and Andrew rowed out from the land and let down their nets once more. This time many, many fish swam into their nets and were caught. The net became so heavy that Simon and Andrew could not pull it out of the water. Quickly they motioned to their partners in the other ship to come and help them. Simon, Andrew, James, and John pulled with all their might. Never had they seen so many fish. Soon both ships were full of fish—so full that the boats began to sink.

Falling at Jesus' knees, Simon cried out, "Leave me, O Lord! for I am a sinful man."

Jesus did not intend to leave Simon. He answered, "Do not be afraid. From now on you will catch men."

Fishermen Leave Their Nets

Matthew 4:18-22; Mark 1:16-38

As Jesus walked by the Sea of Galilee, he saw Andrew and Simon fishing. He called to them, "Follow me and I will make you fishers of men." Immediately they left their boats and followed him.

As the three walked along the shore, they saw two other fishermen mending their nets. These brothers, James and John, were partners with Simon and Andrew in the fishing business. Jesus called James and John to follow him also. At once they left their ship to follow Jesus.

With the four fishermen, Jesus returned to Caper'naum. On the

Sabbath they went to the synagogue. Many people came to hear Jesus. When he spoke they felt as if God was talking to them.

In the crowd was a man who had a very bad spirit. The bad spirit made the man call out, "Let us alone! What do we have to do with you, Jesus of Nazareth? I know you are the Holy One from God."

Jesus said to the bad spirit, "Hold your peace, and come out of him." And the bad spirit came out.

How surprised the people were! Never before had they seen anyone with such power. They said to one another, "What is this? What new teaching? Jesus even commands evil spirits and they obey him!"

Jesus and the four fishermen left the synagogue and went to the home of Simon and Andrew. There they learned that Simon's mother-in-law was sick with a fever. They brought Jesus to her. Taking hold of her hand, he lifted her up. The fever left at once. She got up and helped get the meal.

For the Jews the Sabbath ended at sunset, and they began their work again. When the sun set on this Sabbath, Simon and Andrew saw many people coming toward their home. Some came with crippled friends leaning on their arms. Others led the blind or carried the sick. All wanted Jesus to make their friends and loved ones well.

What a busy time followed! Jesus was glad to help the people. He healed many that night.

When the last group left Simon's house, Jesus lay down to sleep. He must have been very tired, but after sleeping only a few hours he got up quietly and left the city. He found a place where he could be alone to talk with his heavenly Father. Jesus prayed for strength and help to do the great work he had to do.

At daylight more people came to Simon's house, asking for Jesus. Simon and his friends found Jesus was not there. They went to look for him and found him at his place of prayer.

"Everyone is looking for you," they said.

Jesus answered, "I must preach the kingdom of God in other cities also, for I am sent to do this great work." So the disciples went with him to other cities in Galilee. Jesus taught in the synagogues and healed the sick. Many believed in him.

31

Jesus Calls Matthew

Matthew 9:9-13; Mark 2:14-17; Luke 5:27-32

In the land where Jesus lived there was one group of Jews who were hated and despised. They were the publicans, the tax collectors, who worked for the Roman government. The Jews wanted to be an independent nation with their own ruler. They resented the Romans and anyone who worked with the Roman government.

It was the publicans' job to collect from the Jews the taxes levied by the Roman government. Often the publicans took more money than the government charged. In this way they stole from the people and became rich themselves.

Not all publicans robbed the people by taking too much tax money. Because some did, the people thought all tax collectors were dishonest. For that reason the people called them sinners.

One day Jesus walked along a street in the city of Capernaum. There he saw Matthew sitting at a publican's table, collecting tax money from the people. Even though many Jews hated Matthew, Jesus knew that Matthew had a good heart, that he would make a good disciple. To Matthew he said, "Follow me."

Gladly Matthew left his money table and followed Jesus. As Matthew walked away, he thought about his many friends who would like to see Jesus. How much Matthew wanted them to hear Jesus' words!

At his home Matthew gave a great banquet. He invited many friends who were also tax collectors. Jesus and his disciples were the guests of honor.

Even though they had not been invited, the proud scribes and Pharisees gathered in the courtyard of Matthew's house. They watched the dinner party and talked to each other about what they saw. They criticized Jesus for being with these publicans and sinners. No good Jew would do such a thing.

Finally the scribes and Pharisees called Jesus' disciples aside and asked, "Why does your Master eat and drink with publicans and sinners?"

Jesus heard what the proud Jews had said. He answered, "Those who are well do not need a doctor, but the people who are sick. I

Jesus calls to Matthew,
"Follow me."

have not come to call the righteous people, but I have come to call sinners to repent."

The scribes and Pharisees thought they were too righteous to need repentance. The publicans and sinners admitted they had done wrong. Many of them listened to Jesus' words and repented of their sins.

Matthew, the publican, became a true disciple. One of the books in the New Testament is called the Gospel According to Matthew. It records more of Jesus' words than does any of the other Gospels.

The Cripple at the Pool of Bethesda

John 5:1-18

In Jerusalem was a pool called Bethes'da. At times the waters of this pool were strangely moved. The people believed that the first person to step into the water when it was moved would be healed.

No wonder so many sick, crippled, and blind came to wait for the water to move. Five porches had been built beside the pool so these people could rest in the shade while they waited. Some had been coming here for a long time, hoping to be healed when the water was troubled.

Perhaps many were too sick to move quickly when they saw the water bubble up. Perhaps they got so tired watching that they did not see the action when it began. Since only the first person in was made well, many people were always disappointed.

One Sabbath Jesus walked through the porches beside the pool. He saw all the people who had come for healing. Lying on a mat was a crippled man who had not walked for thirty-eight years. Jesus looked down at him and asked gently, "Would you like to be made well?"

The man answered, "Sir, I have no one to help me into the water when it is troubled. Before I can crawl down, someone else steps in."

"Rise up," Jesus said. "Take your bed and walk!"

The surprised man felt strength filling his weakened body. He stood on his feet. At first it was hard for him to believe that he was really well again. Then he stooped down and rolled up his mat.

When he turned to speak to Jesus, Jesus was gone. Picking up his mat, the man started home. How happy he was!

As he walked along carrying his bed mat, people looked at him strangely. The Jews believed it was a sin to carry anything on the Sabbath. Some stopped and reminded him, "This is the Sabbath. It is not right for you to carry your bed."

The man answered, "The one who healed me said, 'Take up your bed and walk.' "

His answer excited the people. Quickly they asked, "Who told you to do this?" How angry they were that someone told this man to break the Sabbath! Because the poor man did not know who Jesus was, he could not answer.

Not long afterwards the man who had been healed went to the temple to worship God. There Jesus found him and said, "Now you are well. Sin no more lest something worse happen to you."

At once the man knew it was Jesus who had made him well. He felt so happy and thankful that he told everyone how Jesus had healed him at the pool of Bethesda.

This only made the leaders more angry! Not only had the man carried his bed, but he had been healed on the Sabbath. They thought it was more important to keep the Law than for a crippled man to be made well again.

Jesus answered, "My Father is at work and I work."

The Jews were furious when they heard this. They wanted to kill Jesus. Not only had he broken the Sabbath, but he said God was his Father.

And that day Jesus taught all those in the temple about the heavenly Father.

Jesus Heals a Withered Hand

Matthew 12:1-15; Mark 2:23–3:6; Luke 6:1-11

After Jesus had angered the Pharisees by healing a crippled man on the Sabbath, they became Jesus' enemies. From that time on they followed Jesus just to find fault.

One Sabbath Jesus and his disciples walked through a grainfield. The disciples were so hungry that they picked a few ears and ate them. When the Pharisees saw this they said to the Master, "You and your disciples have broken the Sabbath law by gathering food to eat."

Jesus reminded them of the time David went to the tabernacle and ate the bread that belonged only to the priests. God knew David and his men were hungry, so he did not punish David. "Even the priests and the Levites work on the Sabbath, offering sacrifices in the morning and the evening," said Jesus. "The Son of man is Lord even of the Sabbath." And he went on to the city to teach in the synagogue.

As he stood up to teach the people, he saw a man who had a withered hand. The Pharisees watched him closely. They hardly knew what this Jesus would do next. The people followed him so willingly that the Pharisees were afraid. They tried to think of clever questions to trick Jesus.

"Is it lawful to heal on the Sabbath?" they asked.

Jesus answered, "If any of you have a sheep and it falls into a pit on the Sabbath, do you not get it out? A man is much more valuable than a sheep! Why then is it not lawful to do good on the Sabbath?"

The Pharisees said no more, but their faces showed how angry they were. Jesus was sorry their hearts were so hard. To the man with the withered hand Jesus said, "Stretch out your hand."

The man obeyed and immediately his hand was healed. The Pharisees were so outraged that they left the synagogue and met to plan a way to kill Jesus.

Jesus knew what the Pharisees were planning. He went out and great crowds followed him. He healed all the sick among them.

The Twelve

Matthew 10:1-4; Mark 3:13-19; Luke 6:12-16

Many people besides the four fishermen and Philip, Nathanael, and Matthew followed Jesus. His teachings were so wonderful that many wanted to be his pupils or disciples. They followed his company from one place to another.

Finally Jesus felt he needed to choose twelve of these men for special training so they could help in his great work. He wanted to send these men to places where he had never gone. They would preach to the people about the kingdom of God.

Even though Jesus knew the hearts of all men, he felt he needed God's help in choosing the Twelve. One night he slipped away quietly and climbed the mountain to pray. There in the quietness he prayed all night for help and wisdom and for strength to do his work.

When morning came Jesus was ready to choose his helpers. Leaving his place of prayer, he joined the company of followers who were waiting in the valley.

From them he chose Simon, whom he called Peter, and Andrew, the brother who first brought Simon to Jesus. Then he chose James and John, the brothers who had been partners with Simon and Andrew in the fishing business. Afterwards he chose Matthew, the publican; Philip, of Bethsaida; Thomas and Bartholomew; another James, who was the son of Alpheus; another Simon, also called Zelotes; Judas, the brother of James; and last of all Judas Iscariot, who finally sold his Lord.

To these twelve men Jesus gave the power to heal. He told them to preach the kingdom of God. These twelve he called apostles which means, "those who are sent out." And Jesus sent out the Twelve to preach to others.

The Sermon on the Mount

Matthew 5–7; Luke 6:17-49

After Jesus had chosen his twelve disciples, he wanted to teach them how to do his work. Up the mountainside they climbed. Then Jesus sat down, and they gathered near to hear him. Many others gathered to hear Jesus too.

Jesus said, "Blessed are the poor in spirit: for theirs is the kingdom of heaven." Perhaps he thought about the proud scribes and Pharisees. The proud will never believe his words and learn how to enter the kingdom of God. Humble people who feel they need God's help to live right Jesus called the "poor in spirit." They are blessed because they shall be given the kingdom of God.

He also said, "Blessed are they that mourn: for they shall be comforted." These words sounded strange. Who ever thought that blessings belong to the troubled and sad? The people did not understand how God loves to comfort his children.

"Blessed are the meek," said Jesus next, "for they shall inherit the earth." He meant that gentle people who control their temper, who try to do the right, will enjoy God's blessings.

Then Jesus said, "Blessed are they which do hunger and thirst after righteousness: for they shall be filled." Perhaps he thought again of the proud Pharisees who believed they were so good that they did not need to repent of their sins and seek God's help. Those who want God's Spirit as much as they want food and drink will be blessed.

"Blessed are they who show mercy to others," said Jesus, "for mercy shall be shown to them. And blessed are they who have pure hearts, for they shall see God. And blessed are those who make peace among men, for they shall be called the children of God." These words the disciples understood; for they knew that God will surely bless people who show understanding love, who do not allow sin to enter their hearts, and who make peace where trouble is.

Then Jesus said, "Blessed are they who are persecuted for the sake of righteousness; for theirs is the kingdom of heaven." People who are persecuted are greatly wronged. After Jesus had been crucified and had risen from the dead, the disciples and other followers learned what it means to be persecuted for righteousness' sake. Jesus said to those who are persecuted, "Rejoice, and be exceeding glad; for great is your reward in heaven."

In this wonderful sermon Jesus taught how Christians should live, how they should pray, how they should treat their enemies and their friends, how God loves and cares for them.

At the close of his sermon, Jesus said, "Those who hear my words and do them are like a wise man who built his house upon the rock. When the rain fell, the floods came, and the winds blew, the house stood strong. But those who hear my words and do not obey them are like a foolish man who built his house upon the sand. When the rain fell, the floods came, and the winds blew, the house fell. Great was the fall of it."

The people looked at each other in surprise. Surely Jesus was the greatest teacher of all. But how could they obey his teachings, "Love your enemies"; "Pray for those who treat you wrongly"; "Do good to those who hate you"? Yet they knew these words sounded like the words of God. Those who loved God wanted to live by these words. God would help them.

Jesus Heals a Leper

Matthew 8:1-4; Mark 1:40-45; Luke 5:12-16

When Jesus and his twelve disciples came down from the mountain, a great crowd followed him. Most of the people had come from the cities and villages in Galilee, but some had even come from Jerusalem and other places in Judea.

Near by stood one poor man who did not dare press into the crowd. How much he needed to be healed of leprosy! He was not allowed to live among his friends and relatives for fear they would catch the disease. He was not allowed to get close enough to touch anyone who was not a leper. What an unhappy life!

The poor leper thought, "I wonder if this Jesus will heal me." Before anyone could stop him, he ran to Jesus, knelt at his feet, and worshiped him. Looking up at Jesus, the man said, "If you are willing, I know you can heal me."

Jesus looked down at the man kneeling at his feet. Great pity and love filled his heart. Jesus knew this man was dying by inches. No doctor could cure this dreaded leprosy. Jesus knew too the many unhappy days this poor man had spent away from his home and loved ones. He knew how lonely a leper was.

Jesus was not afraid to touch this poor man. Kindly he laid his hand on the leper and said, "I am willing. You are healed now."

Quickly the man jumped to his feet. The weary look was gone from his eyes. The man's face was all smiles. Now he was well! How thankful he felt! At first it was hard to believe he had been healed, but when he looked at his skin, there was no sign of leprosy.

In God's law that Moses gave to the people the Lord commanded lepers to offer sacrifices of thanksgiving when they were healed. Jesus reminded the man, "Do not tell anyone about this, but go and show yourself to the priests and offer the sacrifice that Moses commanded."

The man was so happy and thankful for what Jesus had done that he could not keep quiet about it. He had to tell his friends. His friends told their friends, and so the news spread far and wide.

Everyone talked about this great miracle. Many left their homes to follow Jesus. So many people flocked to see and hear him that he could no longer enter the cities. From then on he spent much of his time in the country, and the people came to him there.

A Roman Captain Shows Great Faith

Matthew 8:5-13; Luke 7:1-10

Jesus returned with his disciples to Caper'naum, where he had healed many sick people at the close of one Sabbath. News of his coming reached the city before he arrived. Friends were glad to hear this news.

Other people besides those who knew him were glad to hear of his coming. One of them was a Roman centurion, a captain over one hundred Roman soldiers.

This captain was friendly toward the Jews. He had even built a synagogue for them, perhaps the very one in which Jesus had often taught the people on the Sabbath. Because of his kindness the Jews honored him.

One day a servant of the centurion became sick. On the next day he grew worse until it seemed that he could not live much longer. The centurion loved his servant.

Now the centurion had heard about the sick people whom Jesus had healed. He knew Jesus could heal his servant, but he felt too unworthy to go to Jesus. So he sent the Jewish teachers in the synagogue to ask Jesus to heal the sick servant.

When these Jewish teachers came to Jesus, they told him about the centurion's servant. They told him also about the kindness of this Roman captain and how he had built their synagogue. "He is a worthy man," they said, "for he loves our nation."

40

Jesus went with them. As they neared the centurion's home, they saw men coming to meet them. These friends had been sent to tell Jesus that he need not come into the house to heal the sick man. The centurion did not feel worthy to have Jesus enter his house, and he felt himself too unworthy to go out to meet Jesus. So he sent his friends to carry this message: "Lord, do not trouble yourself to come into my house, for I am not worthy to receive so great a man as you are. Just speak the word, and my servant will be made well. I know you have the power to command sickness to depart, just as I have power to command my soldiers to obey me."

When Jesus heard these words, he was greatly pleased. There was a crowd of curious people following, hoping to see another miracle. He turned to them and said, "Nowhere among the Jews have I found such great faith in me as this captain has shown."

When the friends returned to the house, they found the servant healed.

Four Men Tear Up a Roof

Matthew 9:2-8; Mark 2:1-12; Luke 5:18-26

Wherever Jesus went, crowds followed him. They gathered around him in the streets and in the homes where he stayed. Some of these people were his friends; others were merely curious to hear him speak and to see him do some miracle; others followed to find fault with him.

One day while Jesus was in Caper'naum, many people came to the house where he was staying. Disciples, friends, curiosity seekers, and faultfinders crowded the house until not another person could get inside the door.

Jesus healed those who were sick and preached about the kingdom of God. As the people listened, they heard strange noises overhead. Presently the roof began to part, and the people saw a man lying on a cot being lowered from the ceiling.

From the roof the crippled man's four friends looked on anxiously. Would Jesus heal their crippled friend? He was not able to move about. Day after day he had lain weak and helpless on his bed. His friends had tried to bring him to Jesus, but they could not get

41

through the door because of the crowd. They had to find another way.

When the four carriers could not get through the door, they took the crippled man up onto the roof. Laying down the bed mat, they got down on their knees and began lifting out the tiles of the roof. Soon they could see Jesus preaching below. They tied ropes about the sick man's bed and lowered him very carefully into the room before Jesus.

The people in the room wondered what was happening. They wondered what Jesus would do. Perhaps some of them knew the sick man. How surprised they were to hear Jesus say, "Son, be of good cheer, for your sins are forgiven"!

Now the people did not watch the sick man any longer. Instead they looked at Jesus in surprise. He had dared to say, "Your sins are forgiven." They knew God could forgive sins, but they did not know that Jesus was the Son of God.

The scribes and Pharisees who had come to find fault said in their hearts, "Who is this Jesus who pretends to forgive sins? None except God can do that!"

Jesus knew their thoughts and said, "Why do you think evil of me in your hearts? Is it easier to tell the man that his sins are forgiven, or to tell him to rise up from his bed and walk? But that you may know I have power on earth to forgive sins too"—Jesus said to the man—"Arise, take up your bed, and return to your own house."

Immediately all the stiffness left the sick man's body and his strength returned. He got up, rolled up his bed, and lifted it up onto his shoulders. The people were so surprised that they made way for him as he walked through the room and into the street to join his happy friends.

The people did not know what to think. Some were afraid; all were amazed. They glorified God. As they hurried home, they said to each other, "Surely we have never seen anything like this before!"

A Widow's Son Is Raised to Life

Luke 7:11-17

In the city of Nain in Galilee lived a widow. She had only one child who was now a young man. Proudly the widow had watched her son grow! She thought of the time when he would be able to earn their living.

One day the young man became ill. How worried his mother was! Day after day she sat at his bedside watching for some sign that he was getting better. Tenderly she nursed him, but in spite of all her loving care he grew worse. Then one day he died.

Now the widow was alone. Both her husband and her son were dead and she was very sad and lonely.

Neighbors and friends came to weep with her and plan for the funeral. They wrapped long strips of linen cloth around the lifeless body and placed it on a frame called a bier.

The funeral procession started. In front were the men carrying the bier. Many people followed. The mourners wept aloud as they slowly walked toward the burial place. Suddenly the funeral procession stopped outside the gate. Everyone wondered what had happened. Then they saw a great crowd coming toward them. Walking in front of the crowd were Jesus and his twelve disciples.

When Jesus saw the widow's great sorrow, he wanted very much to help her. He knew the deep ache and loneliness that filled her heart. "Do not weep," he said kindly. Then going over to the bier he said, "Young man, I tell you to arise!"

The young man who had been dead sat up. He began to talk. In speechless surprise those who looked on unwrapped the long linen strips from the young man's body. Then Jesus took him to his mother.

At once the cries stopped and a great silence fell over the people. They could hardly believe their own eyes. Soon they were sure that Jesus had raised the young man to life again. How they rejoiced! "A great prophet is come among us!" they exclaimed. Others cried, "Surely God has visited his people!"

John the Baptist in Prison

Matthew 11:1-6; Luke 3:19-20; 7:18-23

After John baptized Jesus, he continued to preach fearlessly. John even reminded Herod the ruler of his sins, and Herod was very troubled. Herod's wife did not like John the Baptist or his preaching. She wanted her husband to kill this wilderness preacher. To please her, Herod had John the Baptist put in prison.

News of how Jesus raised the widow's son from the dead spread through the country quickly. Even in prison, John the Baptist heard about it. John longed to see and know more about these things. Calling two of his disciples, John said, "Go to Jesus and ask him, 'Are you the one who is to come, or should we look for another?'"

The two hurried to Jesus with John's question. While they waited for Jesus' answer, many people gathered around the Master and begged for healing. There were cripples, blind, lepers, deaf, and people with all kinds of sicknesses. One by one Jesus healed them.

Turning to the two men who had come from John the Baptist, Jesus said, "Go back and tell John what you have seen. Tell him how the blind see, the lame walk, the deaf hear, the lepers are cured, the dead are raised to life, and the evil spirits are cast out. To the poor the glad news of the kingdom is preached."

The two took this message back to John. How glad he was to hear about the wonderful works of Jesus! Not long afterward Herod commanded that John be killed. Friends who had comforted John in prison came and buried his body. Then they went to tell Jesus what Herod had done.

A Woman Anoints Jesus' Feet

Luke 7:36-50

While Jesus taught the people in Galilee, a Pharisee named Simon came to listen. Like many other Pharisees, Simon tried to find fault with Jesus. Because he could find none, he decided to ask Jesus to dinner. During dinner Simon planned to watch Jesus closely to see whether the Master might do something wrong.

44

With her hair the woman wipes her tears from Jesus' feet.

Jesus accepted Simon's invitation and went to his house. Others went too. Some were invited, and some were not. All came into the dining room where the food was spread on the table. The guests took their places around the table, and those who were not invited stood back and looked on.

As was the custom Jesus and the other guests lay on couches facing the table. While they ate, an uninvited woman entered the room. She looked from one guest to another until she saw Jesus. At once she knelt at his feet and wept sorrowfully for her many sins. With her hair she wiped away the tears that fell on his feet. She poured costly perfume on his feet and kissed him.

Simon, the Pharisee, watched the woman. He knew she was a great sinner. Why did Jesus let such a woman weep at his feet? Imagine his surprise when he saw the woman anoint Jesus' feet with costly perfume. In his heart Simon said, "If Jesus were a prophet, he would not allow this woman to come near him. He would know what a sinner she is."

Jesus knew Simon's thoughts. Looking at the proud Pharisee, Jesus said, "Simon, I have something to tell you."

Simon answered very politely, "Master, what is it?"

Then Jesus told him this story: "There was a rich man who loaned money to two poor men. To one he loaned five hundred pence. To the other he loaned fifty. When the time came to pay back the loan neither man had any money. They came to the rich man, and he forgave them both. Which of these two men will love the rich man more?"

"I suppose," answered Simon, "that the man who was forgiven the more will love more."

"You are right," said Jesus. Then he turned to the sinful woman still weeping at his feet and said, "Simon, when I came into your home, you did not treat me like an honored guest. You did not give me water to wash the dust from my feet, but this woman has washed my feet with her tears and dried them with her hair.

"You did not give me a kiss of welcome, but this woman has kissed my feet. You did not anoint my head with oil as you anoint the heads of your friends, but this woman has poured costly perfume on

46

my feet. I tell you that her many sins are forgiven, for she has loved much. Those who have little forgiven, love little."

To the woman Jesus said, "Your sins are forgiven. Your faith has saved you. Go in peace."

Those who looked on said in their hearts, "Who is this man that forgives sins too?"

The Story of the Sower

Matthew 13:1-23; Mark 4:1-20

One day Jesus walked with his disciples beside the seaside outside Caper'naum. Great crowds followed along the beach. They thought Jesus was leaving their city and they wanted to go with him. They crowded so close around Jesus that he stepped into a boat and sat down to teach them.

And Jesus began to teach them by parables. These parables were short stories to show the truths of the gospel. As Jesus sat in the boat he told them about a farmer who went out to sow seeds in his field. This is the story:

"One day a sower took a bag of grain and went out to his field. He walked back and forth across the field scattering handfuls of seed on the ground. As the grain fell the breeze helped scatter it.

"Some seeds blew onto the road. When the birds saw the seeds lying there, they flew down and ate them. Other seeds fell on stony places and began to grow, but the soil was so shallow that the plants soon withered and died. Some seeds fell in thorny places, and the thorns grew so fast that they choked out the good seed.

"But not all the seeds were wasted. Many of them fell on good ground. There they sprouted and sent their roots into the rich soil. After a time they grew into stalks of grain. The stalks produced many more seeds than were first scattered on the ground. Some fields produced thirty times more, others sixty times more, and some even one hundred times more."

The disciples wondered what the story meant. Why was Jesus telling stories instead of preaching sermons? When they climbed back into the boat, they asked him, "Why are you teaching the people with parables?"

47

Jesus answered, "Because I know you will try to find out what the stories mean. Others who hear the stories will not try to understand the meaning because their hearts are not open to God's message."

Then Jesus explained to the disciples what the story of the sower meant.

"The sower," he said, "is the person who speaks the words of God. The different kinds of soil represent the ways people act when they hear God's message. Those who hear it but do not try to understand are like the roadside where the seeds fell. Just as the birds flew down and ate those seeds, the evil one comes and the people forget the message they have heard.

"Those who listen gladly to God's words but do not obey them, are like the stony places. The seeds fell but did not grow because they could not take deep root in the stony soil.

"Those who believe God's word in their hearts but allow trouble, money, or pleasure to crowd it out are like the soil where the thorns choked out the good seeds.

"But those who hear and obey God's word are like the good ground. Here the seeds fell, sprouted, grew into stalks, and produced much grain."

Stories About the Kingdom of Heaven

Matthew 13:24-52; Mark 4:21-34

Jesus told another story to the people. This time he said: "The kingdom of heaven is like a man who sowed good seeds in his field. At night when everyone was asleep, his enemy came and scattered weed seeds everywhere. Both the good seeds and the weed seeds sprouted and grew.

"When the servants saw the weeds, they came to the man and asked, 'Didn't you sow good seeds in your field? Where did all these weeds come from?'

"The man answered, 'An enemy has sown the weeds.'

" 'Shall we pull out the weeds?' the servants asked.

" 'No,' said the master, 'wait until the time for the harvest. If

48

"One day a sower went
out to his field."

you pull up the weeds now, you will pull up the wheat with them. When the wheat is ripe, I will send reapers to gather the weeds, tie them in bundles, and burn them. Then they will gather the wheat and put it in my barn.' "

Next Jesus said, "The kingdom of heaven is like a grain of mustard seed. A man planted it in his field, and it became the tallest thing there. Even the birds came and made nests in its branches."

The women listened more closely when they heard Jesus say, "The kingdom of heaven is also like leaven or yeast that a woman puts into the dough when she is mixing bread. The yeast works through all the dough and causes it to rise."

At last. Jesus sent the people away. Then the disciples asked, "Tell us the meaning of the story about the weeds and the good seeds."

Jesus said, "The good seeds are the people of God, and the weeds are the evil people. Someday God will separate the evil from the good, just as the farmer separates the weeds from his wheat."

Jesus Calms the Storm

Matthew 8:23-27; Mark 4:35-41; Luke 8:22-25

Jesus spent all day teaching the people by the Sea of Galilee. When evening came, he said to his disciples, "Let us cross over to the other side." The disciples and Jesus went in one boat. Some who saw them leave the shore got into their own little boats and followed.

When they were far out from shore, a storm came up. Great waves dashed against the boat. The disciples pulled at the oars with all their might, but it did no good. If the boat were broken to pieces, they would never see land again.

Several disciples knew the sea well. They had seen it rage before, but this time they were completely helpless in the power of the storm.

What should they do? Just then a great wave swept over the boat and flooded it with water. Now the boat would sink. How afraid they were!

50

Jesus was so tired from teaching the people all day that he had fallen asleep. The storm didn't seem to bother him a bit.

At first the disciples did not want to wake him. They knew how tired he was. Now that the boat was about to sink, they ran to him and cried out, "Master, don't you care if we die in this storm?"

Jesus opened his eyes and looked into their frightened faces. He asked, "Why are you so afraid? Don't you have any faith?"

As the disciples watched, Jesus stood up and spoke to the wind and the sea, "Peace, be still." At the sound of his voice the storm stilled. The sea became quiet and calm.

How amazed the disciples were! They asked one another, "What kind of man is he that even the wind and the sea obey him?" And they thought much about the Master's great power.

Jesus Heals a Wild Man

Matthew 8:28-34; Mark 5:1-20; Luke 8:26-39

After the storm was stilled, Jesus and his disciples went ashore in the country of the Gadarenes. Near by was a cemetery where a wild man lived. No chains were strong enough to hold him. Night and day he wandered in this lonely place, crying and cutting himself with stones.

From a distance the wild man saw Jesus. At once he ran, fell at Jesus' feet, and worshiped him. The evil spirits that troubled him as with one voice called out to Jesus, "What have I to do with you, Jesus, Son of the most high God? I beg you, do not torment me."

Jesus knew the man could never be well so long as he was filled with evil spirits. Jesus said, "Come out of the man, you unclean spirit." Then he asked the man, "What is your name?"

The evil spirit replied, "My name is Legion, for we are many."

On a mountainside near by was a herd of two thousand hogs with the servants who took care of the animals. The evil spirits said to Jesus, "Send us into the hogs."

"Go," Jesus answered.

At once the great herd ran down the mountainside, plunged into the sea, and all the hogs were drowned. How frightened the servants were when they saw this! Away they ran to the city to tell what had happened.

Soon a crowd of curious people gathered. They were much surprised to see the wild man sitting at Jesus' feet, wearing clothes, and acting perfectly well. A peaceful look was on his face, and he had the right use of his mind again.

The people were afraid. What kind of man was Jesus? A whole herd of hogs had been drowned on account of him. What if he did more things like that in their country? They did not even think of bringing their sick for him to heal. Instead they begged him to go away and leave them alone.

Jesus and his disciples returned to their boat, and the man who had been healed followed. He wanted to go with them, but Jesus said, "Go back to your home and tell your friends what great things the Lord has done for you."

Gladly the man obeyed. From city to city he went, telling people about the wonderful power of Jesus.

Jesus Answers Calls for Help

Matthew 9:18–10:42; Mark 5:22-43; Luke 8:41–9:6

Jesus and his disciples had just returned by ship to Caper'naum. An eager crowd waited on the shore to welcome them. And again Jesus taught them and healed the sick.

A man came running to Jesus. He fell down at Jesus' feet and cried, "My daughter is dying; but if you will come and lay your hands on her, she will be made well."

This man was Ja'irus, a ruler of the synagogue in Capernaum. Perhaps Jesus knew Jairus, for he had taught often in the synagogue. At once Jesus started to go with the man to heal his daughter. The disciples went too, and the crowd followed, eager to see another miracle. As they went, the people pressed close to Jesus.

In this crowd was a poor woman who had been ill for twelve years. She had spent all her money on doctors, yet they did not help her. Now she had no more money. Hearing about Jesus' power to heal, she decided to go to him and be made well.

Jesus said,
"Little girl, get up!"

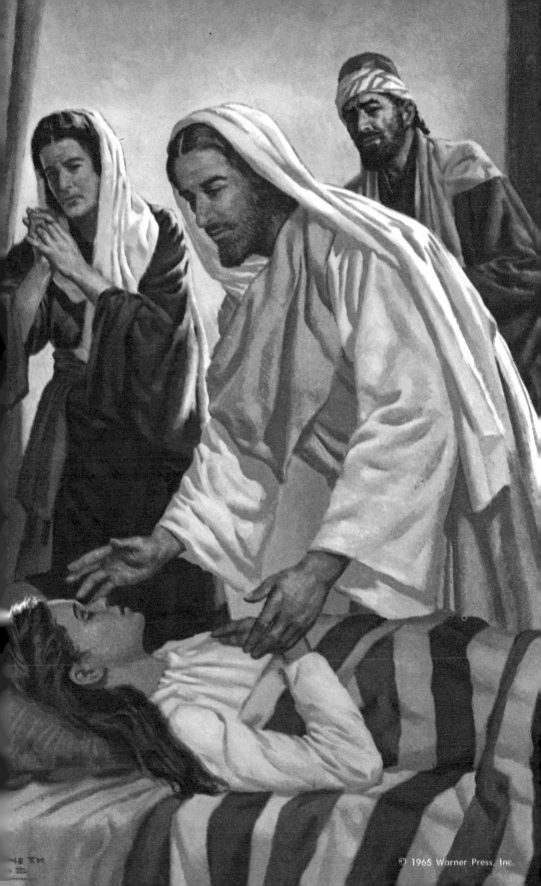

How hard it was to reach him! But she pressed her way through the crowd till she came very near. In her heart she thought, "I need not ask him to make me well; if only I can touch the hem of his coat, I shall be healed." So she edged her way closer, until she could reach out her hand and touch Jesus' clothes. Immediately she was healed, and she stepped back into the crowd.

But Jesus knew what the woman had done. Turning around he asked, "Who touched me?"

Amazed, the disciples asked, "Why do you ask who touched you when the people are pressing against you from every side?"

But Jesus answered, "Someone has touched me, for I felt healing power go from my body."

The woman came trembling and fell down before him. Jesus spoke to her kindly, "Daughter, your faith has made you well; go in peace."

Jairus stood by waiting impatiently for Jesus to come to his house. What if his daughter died before they reached her bedside? And sure enough, a servant came with the sad news, "Do not trouble the Master any longer, for it is too late."

Jesus heard the message and knew how Jairus felt. He said, "Do not be afraid; only believe, and she shall yet be made well." So on they went.

At the ruler's house many friends and neighbors had gathered to weep with the sorrowing mother. Jesus asked, "Why do you weep? The girl is not dead but sleeping." They laughed at him, for they knew the girl was dead.

Then Jesus sent everyone out of the room except the father and the mother and Peter, James, and John. Taking the girl's hand, he said, "Little girl, get up!" At his command she opened her eyes, got up, and walked about the room.

Jesus told her parents, "Give her food to eat." He asked that they tell no one what he had done. News of this miracle would only draw greater crowds than ever.

When they left the home of Jairus, two blind men followed Jesus, crying, "O Son of David, have mercy on us!" They followed him into the house where he was staying.

Jesus asked, "Do you believe that I am able to open your blind eyes?"

Quickly they answered, "Yes, Lord."

Touching their eyes, Jesus said, "Let it be done to you just as you believe." And their eyes were opened.

So great were the crowds that came to hear Jesus that he could not teach them all. Sending his twelve disciples to other cities, he told them to preach the gospel and heal the sick. The work was too great for Jesus to do alone.

A Boy's Lunch Basket

Matthew 14:13-23; Mark 6:30-46; Luke 9:10-17; John 6:1-15

The disciples returned to Jesus, telling about the people they had healed and taught in Galilee. Now more and more people heard about Jesus. They came from everywhere to hear and see him.

The people were so eager to hear Jesus and have their loved ones healed, that they were always with him. He did not have time to rest or even to eat. So Jesus called his twelve disciples to him and said, "Come with me to a quiet place, for we must rest awhile."

They sailed to the other side of the sea and went into a desert place. But they did not find much time to rest, for soon a great crowd gathered. The people had followed from the other side of the sea. Perhaps the disciples were disappointed because the people had found them again, but Jesus looked at the people lovingly. "They are like sheep that have no shepherd," he said.

Jesus sat down to teach them again. He healed the sick and taught the people about the kingdom of heaven.

Evening came. Still the people stayed. They seemed to forget they could not find food or shelter in the desert. The disciples wanted Jesus to send the people away. "Send the people away," said the disciples, "so they can buy food in the towns and villages as they go home."

But Jesus answered, "We must feed them before sending them away." Turning to Philip, he asked, "Where shall we find bread, that all these people may eat?"

Philip looked at the people and shook his head. "If we should buy two hundred pennyworth of bread," he answered, "there would not be enough for each one to have a small piece."

In this great crowd were five thousand men besides all the women and children. When they left home, they did not know they would have to go so far to find Jesus. One boy, however, had not forgotten his lunch basket. In it were five little loaves of barley bread and two small fishes.

The boy heard Jesus and the disciples talking about what to do. He went up to Andrew, showed his lunch basket, and offered to give the food to Jesus. Andrew told Jesus.

"How many loaves are there in the basket?" asked Jesus.

"Only five and two small fishes," Andrew said. "But what will that be among so many people?"

"Bring it to me," Jesus replied. To the disciples he said, "Make the people sit down in groups of fifty and a hundred."

Jesus took the loaves and fishes, gave thanks, and broke the food into small pieces. He filled a basket for each disciple to pass among the hungry people.

When the crowd had eaten all they wanted, Jesus had the disciples gather up the food that was left. There were twelve baskets full.

This miracle excited the people. They wanted Jesus to become their king. How wonderful it would be to have a king who could feed them by working miracles!

Jesus would not allow the people to make him king. He had not come to the earth to rule an earthly kingdom. He commanded his disciples to enter the ship and return to the other side of the sea. Sending the people away, he went alone up the mountainside to pray.

Jesus Walks on the Water

Matthew 14:23-36; Mark 6:47-56; John 6:16-29

After spending the day with Jesus, the people walked along the northern shore of the sea to their homes. The disciples climbed into their boat and started to row toward Caper'naum. Jesus went up the mountain to pray alone.

After nightfall a strong wind blew across the sea and beat against the little boat. The disciples rowed with all their might, but they could not make much progress against the wind. Higher and higher the waves dashed and rolled. The little boat could not plow through them.

How tired the disciples became! They must have remembered the time Jesus was with them and stilled the storm. If only he were with them now!

Far away on the mountain Jesus had prayed for several hours. When the storm came up, he knew how much his disciples needed him. He would go to them at once. Out across the water he walked, just as easily as if it had been land. Nearer and nearer he came to the tossing ship.

The disciples looked up and saw a person walking on the waves. How frightened they were! Each disciple thought he had seen a spirit, for surely no man could walk on the water. In fear they cried out.

When Jesus heard their cry, he said, "Do not be afraid, for it is I."

The voice was familiar, but still the disciples could scarcely believe it was Jesus. Finally Simon Peter called out, "Lord, if it is you, tell me to come to you walking on the water."

And Jesus answered, "Come."

With a bound Simon Peter leaped over the side of the ship and started to Jesus. The other disciples looked on in amazement. What great power Jesus had!

A strong wind blew against Peter, and he was afraid. He looked at the waves and began to sink. "Lord, save me!" he cried out.

Jesus reached out his hand and caught Peter. "O man of little faith, why did you doubt?" Jesus asked.

The two climbed into the boat, and the others rejoiced. At once the wind stopped. Again the disciples marveled at the Master's great power. They worshiped him, saying, "Surely you are the Son of God."

When morning came, the people who had been with Jesus the day before went to find him again. They had seen the disciples leave in their boat. But Jesus had stayed behind. The people looked everywhere, but they could not find him. Finally they sailed across the Sea of Galilee to Capernaum in their search for Jesus.

At Gennes'aret near Capernaum they found the Master. Here, too, crowds of people from this region gathered around him. They brought with them those who were sick.

Wherever Jesus went, in villages or cities or in the country, the people laid the sick in the road he would travel. They believed the sick would be healed if they could even touch the hem of his robe. And those who did, were healed.

A Gentile Mother Comes to Jesus

Matthew 15:21-28; Mark 7:24-30

Near Galilee was the small country of Phoeni'cia. The people who lived there were Gentiles. Many of them worshiped idols. Since they lived so close to Galilee, they knew about the Jewish religion too.

So many people followed Jesus that he could not find time to be alone with his disciples. Perhaps he would have more time to teach his friends if he left Galilee. And so Jesus took his disciples and went to the neighboring country of Phoenicia.

But even the Phoenicians had heard about Jesus. They were eager to see him. News of his coming spread throughout the region. Even in a strange land Jesus could not hide himself.

In this region there was a poor Gentile mother who was very sad. Her little girl was tormented by an evil spirit. This worried mother had heard that Jesus could cast out evil spirits and restore people to their right minds. As soon as she learned that Jesus was near by, she left her work and ran to find him.

When she reached Jesus, she pleaded, "Have mercy on me, O Lord, Son of David, for my daughter is very ill."

Jesus did not seem to hear the woman. He paid no attention to her request. Still the woman followed, begging for his help. The disciples were annoyed at her. Scorning her, they told Jesus, "Send her away, for she calls after us."

58

Perhaps the woman was afraid Jesus would do that. At once she fell at his feet and worshiped him. "Lord, help me," she begged.

The loving heart of Jesus was touched. He wanted to help this poor woman. To test her faith he answered, "I am not sent to the Gentiles, but to the lost children of Israel. It is not right to take the children's bread and throw it to dogs."

The proud Jews called the Gentiles "dogs." The woman understood that Jesus referred to the Jews and the Gentiles. She did not mind being called a dog if only her daughter could be healed.

She said, "I know the children's bread should not be given to the dogs, but the dogs eat the crumbs that fall from the children's table." As a Gentile, the woman wanted a crumb of healing for her child.

Jesus did not make the woman wait any longer for his answer. He was so pleased with her faith and her wise words that he said, "O woman, you have great faith. Go back home, for your daughter is well."

Gladly the woman jumped to her feet and obeyed Jesus. She was sure her child was well. When she reached home, the little girl was lying on the bed, resting quietly. The evil spirit was gone.

Jesus Heals and Feeds the Crowd

Matthew 15:29-39; Mark 7:31—8:10

Leaving Phoeni'cia, Jesus and his twelve disciples passed through the country where Jesus had once healed a wild man called Legion. When Jesus healed him, the evil spirits entered a herd of hogs that was near by. The hogs ran down the mountainside, plunged into the sea, and were drowned. Because of this the people had begged Jesus to leave.

On this second visit things were different. The man who had been made well had returned to his home and told everyone about Jesus. Everywhere he told people that the power of Jesus had cured him. They listened with interest. Before they had been afraid of this man Legion, but now he was changed. The people were sorry they had sent Jesus away.

When Jesus returned, the people flocked to see and hear him.

They followed him into the country. For three days they listened to his teachings. They brought to him their lame, blind, dumb, crippled, and sick. Jesus healed every one of them.

Among those that were brought for healing was a man who could not hear or talk. Jesus took the man aside from the crowd. Putting his fingers in the man's ears and touching his tongue, Jesus looked up to heaven and said, "Be opened!"

Immediately the man could hear and speak. He was so happy and thankful that he could not keep from telling what Jesus had done. Jesus asked him and the people who saw him not to tell about the healing. The people were so astonished that they said: "Jesus does all things well. He makes both the deaf to hear and the dumb to speak."

The evening of the third day Jesus called his disciples aside and reminded them, "I feel sorry for all these people. They have been with me three days, and they have nothing to eat. If I send them home now, they will faint by the way. Many live far away."

The disciples agreed, but they asked, "How can we feed such a crowd out here in the desert?"

"How many loaves do you have?" Jesus asked.

And they told him, "Only seven, and a few small fish."

Jesus turned to the people and commanded them to sit down. When they had obeyed, he gave thanks for the loaves and fish.

Just as when he fed the five thousand from the boy's lunch, these few loaves and fish became enough food for every one. More than four thousand people were fed. Seven baskets of food were left over.

Now Jesus dismissed the crowd. They started home. Among them were the sick who had been made well. How glad the people were that Jesus had visited their country this second time!

In a boat Jesus and his disciples crossed to the other side of the Sea of Galilee.

Jesus feeds the
great crowd.

The Blind Man of Bethsaida

Mark 8:22-26

Near Bethsa'ida, a town by the Sea of Galilee, lived a blind man. He had never been to Jesus, but he had heard that the Master healed all who were brought to him. The blind man wished that he too could be healed.

One day someone told the blind man that Jesus and his twelve friends were in Bethsaida. "I must go to Jesus at once," the blind man said. And friends led him to the place where Jesus was staying.

Jesus did his best not to attract any more crowds. He knew the time of his ministry was growing short. He must train the disciples so they could carry on his work after he was gone. He needed to spend time alone with them.

Friends of the blind man asked Jesus to heal his eyes. Jesus took the man by the hand and led him outside the town. When the two were alone, Jesus touched the blind eyes and asked, "Can you see?"

At first things looked blurred to the man. He answered, "I see men that look like trees walking."

Again Jesus touched the man's eyes and his sight was restored. The man saw everything clearly.

Jesus said, "Do not go into the town or tell any of the townspeople what I have done for you."

And the man who had been blind went on his way rejoicing.

Peter's Great Confession

Matthew 16:13-28; Mark 8:27—9:1; Luke 9:18-27

Jesus and his disciples traveled north to the city of Caesare'a Philippi. On the way Jesus questioned the disciples. First he asked, "Who do people say that I am?"

The disciples answered, "Some say you are Eli'jah, the prophet, come back to earth. Some think you are John the Baptist risen from the dead. Others believe you are Jeremi'ah or another prophet who taught long ago."

Next Jesus asked, "But who do you say that I am?"

Boldly Simon Peter answered, "You are the Christ, the Son of the living God."

Jesus rejoiced to hear this. At least his disciples understood who he was. Jesus charged them not to tell this to anyone.

Then Jesus talked about the troubles and sorrows that would come to him at Jerusalem. He would be arrested and cruelly treated. Because the elders, chief priests, and scribes would reject him, he would be killed. After three days he would rise again.

The disciples did not understand what Jesus meant. They believed he would soon be their king, and they would have important places in his kingdom. Why should he talk about dying now?

Simon Peter, who often spoke for all the Twelve, took Jesus aside and said, "These terrible things must never happen to you."

Jesus turned and looked sadly at his disciples. To Peter he said, "You talk like Satan, the tempter. You do not understand the things of God; you understand only the things of men."

How much easier it would have been for Jesus to accept a throne and an earthly kingdom than to suffer and die! But Jesus did not want to do anything just because it was easy. He wanted to do his Father's will.

Later Jesus gathered the people and his disciples around him and told them what it meant to be his follower. "If anyone wants to follow me, he must not live his own way but my way. He must not be selfish and try only to take care of himself. If he will let his life be used entirely for my sake and for the gospel's, he will be saved. What is a man profited if he gains the whole world and loses his own soul? Or what will a man give in exchange for his soul? God will reward every man for what he does."

The people marveled at Jesus' teachings.

The Mount of Transfiguration

Matthew 17:1-13; Mark 9:2-13; Luke 9:28-36

After a long hard climb up a rough mountain slope near Caesare'a Philippi, the three disciples were tired. Far above the quiet valley Simon Peter, James, and John looked for a place to rest. These fishermen were more used to rowing a boat than climbing a mountain. Jesus had asked them to go with him to the mountain to pray.

When the three disciples reached the top, they were too tired to pray. They fell asleep, and Jesus prayed alone.

While they slept, a great change came over the Master. His face shone as bright as the sun, and his clothing gleamed whiter than anything on earth. Two men came from heaven to talk with him. One was Moses who had written down God's law, and the other was Eli'jah who had spoken God's words to Israel. The three talked of Jesus' coming death.

The three were still talking when the disciples woke up. How amazed they were to see their Master clothed in such glory! In astonishment they watched as he talked with Moses and Elijah.

As Moses and Elijah were leaving, Simon Peter exclaimed, "Lord, it is good for us to be here! If you are willing, let us build three tabernacles—one for you, one for Moses, and one for Elijah."

While Peter spoke, a cloud overshadowed the disciples and they were afraid. From the cloud a voice said, "This is my beloved Son, in whom I am well pleased. Hear him."

The disciples fell to the ground, trembling with fear. Jesus came near, laid his hands on them, and said, "Get up. Do not be afraid."

The disciples looked around and saw only Jesus. The cloud and the heavenly visitors were gone. Now they believed surely that Jesus was the Son of God.

The next day they climbed down the mountain. Jesus told them not to tell anyone about what had happened until after he had risen from the dead. Still the disciples wondered why he talked about pain and death when he, the Son of God, had been in such heavenly glory on the mountain.

Later when all the disciples were together, they asked, "Why do our teachers say that Elijah must come before the Messiah appears?"

Jesus answered, "Elijah has already come, but they did not know him. They went on doing just as they pleased. They will make the Son of man suffer also."

The disciples understood that Jesus was referring to John the Baptist who had been imprisoned and killed. Meanwhile a crowd gathered in the valley to see Jesus.

Jesus Heals an Epileptic Boy

Matthew 17:14-21; Mark 9:14-29; Luke 9:37-43

Jesus and his three disciples left the Mount of Transfiguration and started back to the valley. They found the other nine disciples surrounded by a questioning crowd.

When Jesus came near, a man ran out of the crowd and fell at his feet. "Lord, have mercy on my only son," he pleaded. "He has spells and falls down. Sometimes he has fallen into the fire or into the water. I brought him to your disciples, but they could not help."

Jesus was greatly disappointed that his disciples did not have enough faith to heal the boy. "O faithless generation," Jesus said sadly, "how long shall I be with you? How long shall I put up with you?" Turning to the troubled father, Jesus said, "Bring your child to me."

As they brought him, the boy had an attack. He fell to the ground, lay in the dust, and foamed at the mouth.

"How long has your son been this way?" Jesus asked.

The father answered, "Ever since he was a small child. Often he has almost lost his life when these attacks came upon him. If you can do anything, have mercy on us and help us."

Jesus knew the father did not have faith in his power to heal the boy. "If you can believe," Jesus told him, "all things are possible to him who believes."

At once the father cried out, "O Lord, I do believe; help me not to doubt."

Jesus commanded the bad spirit to come out of the boy and torment him no longer. The boy lay so quiet on the ground that the people said, "He is dead."

Jesus stooped down, took the boy's hand, and lifted him up. The boy stood on his own feet and walked to his father. He was completely well.

As soon as the disciples could be alone with Jesus, they asked, "Why were we not able to heal the boy?"

"Because you did not have faith," Jesus said. "You cannot help such people unless you live a life of prayer." And he talked to them about their need for faith in God.

Who is the Greatest?

Matthew 17:22—18:14; Mark 9:30-43; Luke 9:43-50

Leaving the north country near Caesare'a Philippi, Jesus and his disciples started back to Caper'naum. On the way Jesus told them, "The Son of man will be delivered into the hands of men. They will kill him, but he will rise again on the third day." The disciples did not understand what Jesus meant, and they were afraid to ask.

As they walked along some of the disciples began to argue about who would be greatest in the kingdom of heaven. They still thought Jesus would set up an earthly kingdom and honor them with high positions.

When they reached Capernaum, Jesus took his disciples to a private home. He did not want to attract the crowds, and few people knew about his stopping place.

While they were in Capernaum, a man who collected tax money for the temple in Jerusalem stopped Simon Peter. He asked the disciple, "Does your master pay taxes?"

"Yes," Peter answered.

When Peter returned to the house where they were staying, he told Jesus about this. Jesus said, "Take your hook and line down to the sea. There will be a piece of money in the mouth of the first fish you catch. Take this and pay our taxes."

Peter obeyed and found the piece of money in the fish's mouth, just as Jesus had said. After paying the tax, Peter returned to the place where they were staying.

When all the disciples were together, Jesus asked them, "What were you arguing about on the way to Capernaum?"

No one answered. They were too ashamed to tell, but Jesus knew what they had talked about as they walked along the dusty road. Jesus said, "If anyone wants to be great, he must serve others." Taking a little child into his arms, he said, "No one can enter the kingdom of heaven unless he becomes like a little child. Whoever is as humble as a little child shall be the greatest in the kingdom of heaven. You must be careful not to do anything that will make a person lose faith in me."

To show the disciples how important each person was, Jesus said,

"If a man has one hundred sheep and one goes astray, does he not leave the ninety and nine and go to look for the one that is lost? When he finds the lost sheep, he is happier over it than over the ninety-nine that are safe in the fold. In the same way your heavenly Father does not want to lose a single person from his kingdom."

Then John told Jesus that some of them had seen a man healing people in Jesus' name. "We told him to stop doing that because he was not one of us."

"You should not have done that," Jesus said. "Whoever does a miracle in my name is helping me in my great work." Jesus must have been discouraged that his disciples understood so little about him and his work.

Peter Learns About Forgiveness

Matthew 18:21-35

One day Simon Peter asked Jesus, "Lord, how often shall I forgive my brother if he sins against me? Shall I forgive him seven times?"

Jesus replied, "I do not say that you shall forgive him seven times only, but seventy times seven."

Peter was surprised. Could he ever forgive a man that many times?

Jesus told Peter a story about a king whose servant owed him much money. The king called this servant and asked him to pay the debt, but the servant could not. The king said, "Because you cannot pay the money you borrowed, I command that you, your wife, and your children be sold, and that all you own be taken away from you. In this way I can get back some of the money you borrowed."

The servant fell on his face before the king, crying, "O King, have patience with me and I will pay every penny I owe!"

Because the king felt sorry for the man, he said, "I will forgive all the debt, and you need not try to pay it back."

When this servant left the king, he met a poor man who had borrowed only a few dollars from him. He asked the man to pay it back, but the man could not. The servant became so angry that he took the poor man by the throat and cried, "Pay back what you borrowed or I will throw you into prison!"

The poor man fell to his knees and pleaded, "Have patience with me, and I will pay every penny I owe."

The king's servant would not listen. Because the poor man had no money, the king's servant threw him into prison.

Other servants of the king felt sad when they saw how unkindly this poor man had been treated, and they told the king.

The king was surprised. Quickly he sent for the unkind servant. In anger the king told him, "O wicked man, I forgave all your debt because you could not pay. Should you not have been willing to forgive the small debt your poor neighbor owed even as I forgave you? Now you will go to prison until you pay all you ever owed."

When Jesus finished the story, he said to Peter, "If you do not forgive from your heart the wrongdoings of others, neither will your heavenly Father forgive you."

On the Way Through Samaria

Luke 9:51-56

Jesus and his disciples were on their way to Jerusalem. They planned to take the road through the country of Samar'ia. At one Samaritan village Jesus planned to spend the night. He sent messengers ahead to find a place for them to stay.

But the Samaritans did not want Jesus and his disciples to stay overnight in their town. Jesus and his disciples were Jews. Because the Jews had often been unkind to the Samaritans, the Samaritans did not want anything to do with the Jews.

James and John were furious that they had been refused lodging for the night. They said, "Lord, why don't you call fire down from heaven on this village?"

Jesus answered, "How wrong you are! The Son of man is not come to destroy men's lives, but to save them." Jesus went on to another village, and his disciples followed.

Jesus teaches his disciples
to be like little children.

The Ten Lepers

Luke 17:11-19

As Jesus and his disciples passed by they met ten men who were lepers. These men had heard that Jesus healed the sick. Because they were lepers they could not go near Jesus. From a distance they called loudly, "Jesus, Master, have mercy on us!"

Never did Jesus pass by and refuse to help one who called. When he saw the lepers, he said, "Go show yourselves to the priests." At once the lepers started to go to the priests for an examination. And as they went the leprosy left their bodies and they were made every bit well.

One of the lepers stopped and turned back when he knew he had been healed. Running to Jesus, he fell down before him, worshiping and thanking him for this miracle. The other nine hurried on their way, never stopping to thank the great healer. Now the man who gave thanks was not a Jew, but a Samar'itan.

Jesus said to his disciples, "Were not ten lepers made well? But where are the nine? None turned back to give thanks except this stranger." Then Jesus said to the man kneeling at his feet, "Rise up and go your way, for your faith has made you well."

Would-Be Followers

Matthew 8:18-22; Luke 9:57-62

As Jesus and his disciples walked along the road, a man said to the Master, "Lord, I would like to follow you wherever you go."

Jesus explained that his followers had many hardships. "Foxes have holes in the ground for their homes, the birds of the air have nests, but the Son of man has no place of his own to lay his head."

They had not gone much farther when Jesus said to a man by the road, "Follow me."

"But my father is old," the man answered. "Let me wait until he dies. Then I will follow you."

"That will be too late," Jesus told him. "You should go now and preach the kingdom of God."

After they had gone on a little distance, another man told Jesus, "Lord, I want to follow you. But first let me go home and spend some time with my relatives."

Jesus answered, "No man who starts to do my work and looks back is fit for the kingdom of God."

None of these men would make good followers, for they did not put Jesus and his work first in their lives.

Jesus Attends the Feast in Jerusalem
John 7:2-53

Summer was over, and the cooler days of autumn had come. On the hillsides around Jerusalem stood groups of booths or huts made from branches. During the Feast of Tabernacles, the Jews lived out of doors. These booths were their only shelter. Visitors came from every part of the land for the feast.

On the first day as people talked together, they wondered if Jesus would come to the feast to teach them. Some told of things they had heard him say. Others talked about his miracles.

As the people talked and asked about Jesus, they expressed different opinions. Some said, "He is a good man." Others replied, "No, he deceives the people." Only in their small groups did the people talk about Jesus. No one dared speak of him publicly. They were afraid of the Jewish rulers.

The people looked for Jesus but he was nowhere to be found. "Where is he?" they asked.

About the middle of the week Jesus came to the temple and taught. His enemies thought this would be a good time to catch him. They sent men to listen to his teaching. These men would find fault with what Jesus said and accuse him before the rulers.

And the men did as they had been ordered. Yet as they listened to the Master, they marveled. "How does this man know so much without having been trained?" they wondered.

Jesus answered, "My teaching is not mine, but his who sent me."

Day after day Jesus sat in the temple, teaching all who came to him. No one tried to send him away, and no one tried to arrest him.

Many Jews who lived in Jerusalem knew how much their leaders hated Jesus. They wondered why the leaders had not seized the Master and thrown him into prison. They said of Jesus, "Is not this the man they are after? Here he is speaking boldly, and they say nothing to him. Do the rulers believe he is the Christ?"

The rulers of the Jews—the chief priests, the scribes, the Pharisees, and the Sad'ducees—did not believe Jesus was the Christ. They were jealous because he was the center of attention at the feast. They hated his teaching because he accused them of only pretending to be righteous. Finally they sent officers to take him.

As the officers listened to Jesus, they heard him say, "I will be with you yet a little while. Then I shall go to him who sent me. You will look for me, but you will not be able to find me. Where I am, you will not be able to come."

When the officers heard this, they asked one another, "Where could he go that we would not be able to find him? Would he go to the Jews who live abroad? Would he go to teach the Gentiles?"

The officers noticed how eagerly the people listened to Jesus. They heard some say, "Truly this is the Prophet," or, "This is the Christ." They heard others question, "Will Christ come from Galilee? According to the Scriptures he will come from Bethlehem and be of the family of David."

Even though the people differed in what they thought of Jesus, the officers were so impressed that they could not arrest him. They listened carefully to his words. Why should this man be punished? they wondered. So they returned to the rulers without Jesus.

The chief priests and Pharisees were angry that the officers had not obeyed orders. "Why have you not brought him?" they asked.

The officers replied, "No man ever spoke like this man," and they refused to harm him.

Then the rulers were all the more angry and excited. They asked, "Are you letting this man deceive you as he deceives the people? Have any of our rulers believed in him? Only the people who do not understand the Law believe him."

72

Jesus' enemies seek
to get rid of him.

Among the angry rulers sat Nicode'mus, the Pharisee who had come to Jesus one night. He loved Jesus and believed in him. In the hope of protecting Jesus, he asked, "Does our law condemn any man before he is given a hearing?"

The angry rulers turned on Nicodemus and replied scornfully, "Are you from Galilee? Don't you know that no prophet comes from that country?" After saying that they dismissed the meeting and went to their homes.

A Sinful Woman is Brought to Jesus

John 8:1-11

Early the next morning the scribes and Pharisees planned another way to get Jesus arrested. They would go to him themselves and ask a very tricky question about the Law of Moses. If he did not agree with the Law of Moses on this thing, the rulers would accuse him of disobeying the Law and making himself greater than Moses.

As Jesus taught in the temple, the scribes and Pharisees brought a sinful woman. They said, "Master, this woman is very wicked. We caught her committing sin. Moses commanded in the Law that such people should be stoned to death. What do you think we ought to do?"

Jesus knew his enemies were trying to trick him. At first he paid no attention to them. Instead he stooped down and wrote in the sand as if he had not heard their question.

How angry the men were that Jesus did not answer! So they asked him again and again.

Finally Jesus stood up and looked them straight in the eyes as he said, "Let the man among you who is without sin throw the first stone at her." Again Jesus stooped down and wrote in the dust.

At first the rulers looked from one to the other. Then as they remembered some of their own sins, they looked away. Some stared at the ground. Their consciences troubled them. One man became so uncomfortable that he left. Soon another followed. One by one they turned and went away.

When Jesus looked up, he saw only the woman there. He asked, "Where are those who accused you? Did no man condemn you?"

And she replied, "No man, Lord."

Then he said, "Neither do I condemn you. Go and sin no more."

Questioned by His Enemies

John 8:12-59

As the people gathered in the temple, Jesus taught them again. "I am the light of the world," Jesus said. "The man who follows me will not walk in darkness. He will have the light of life."

When the Pharisees heard this, they accused him, "Your words are not true. You are just speaking for yourself."

Jesus answered, "It is written in your law that the testimony of two men is true. I witness for myself and the Father who sent me witnesses for me."

The Pharisees knew that Joseph the carpenter was dead, so they asked, "Where is your Father?"

"You do not know me or my Father," Jesus told them. "If you knew me, you would know my Father also."

Jesus continued to teach publicly in the temple. The Pharisees wanted to seize him, yet no one dared lay hands on him.

Later Jesus said, "I go my way, and you will look for me. You will die in your sins. Where I go, you cannot come."

The Jews did not understand what Jesus meant. They whispered to one another, "Does he plan to kill himself? He says where he goes we cannot come."

Knowing their thoughts, Jesus said, "You are from below. I am from above. You are of this world. I am not of this world."

To those who believed on him, Jesus said, "If you do what I command, then you are truly my disciples. You shall not die in sin, but have eternal life."

Angrily Jesus' enemies said, "Now we know you have an evil spirit. Abraham is dead, and all the prophets are dead. Yet you say anyone who obeys your commands will never die. Are you greater than our father Abraham? Who do you think you are?"

Jesus replied, I do not honor myself, but my Father, God, honors me. You do not know my Father, but I know him. If I said I did not, I would be telling a lie. I know him and obey his words. Your father Abraham was glad when he saw my day, but you do not act like the children of Abraham."

At once the Jews cried out, "How could you have seen our father Abraham? You are not even fifty years old!"

"Before Abraham was, I am," Jesus answered.

"I AM" was the name by which God was known long ago. The Jews were struck with horror when they heard Jesus call himself by that sacred name. They picked up stones and would have killed him, but Jesus lost himself in the crowds.

Jesus Heals a Blind Man

John 9

One Sabbath day as Jesus left the temple, he saw a blind man begging by the roadside. This man had been blind since birth. He lived with his parents in Jerusalem.

The disciples had seen him before. They asked, "Master, who sinned that this man was born blind?"

"No one sinned," Jesus told them. "He is blind so the power of God can be shown through him."

The disciples watched as Jesus stopped in front of the blind man. Mixing a little clay, Jesus rubbed it on the blind man's eyelids. "Go, wash in the pool of Silo'am," Jesus told the poor man.

Without a word the blind man arose and groped his way to the pool. Here he washed the mud from his sightless eyes. Immediately he could see, and he ran home to tell the good news.

Everyone was surprised when he told what had happened! Some who saw him asked, "Is this the man who sat by the roadside and begged?" To this some said, "This is he." Others replied, "It looks like him."

The man who had been blind settled the question by saying, "I am he."

The excitement grew when the people heard that Jesus had opened

Jesus heals a man
blind since birth.

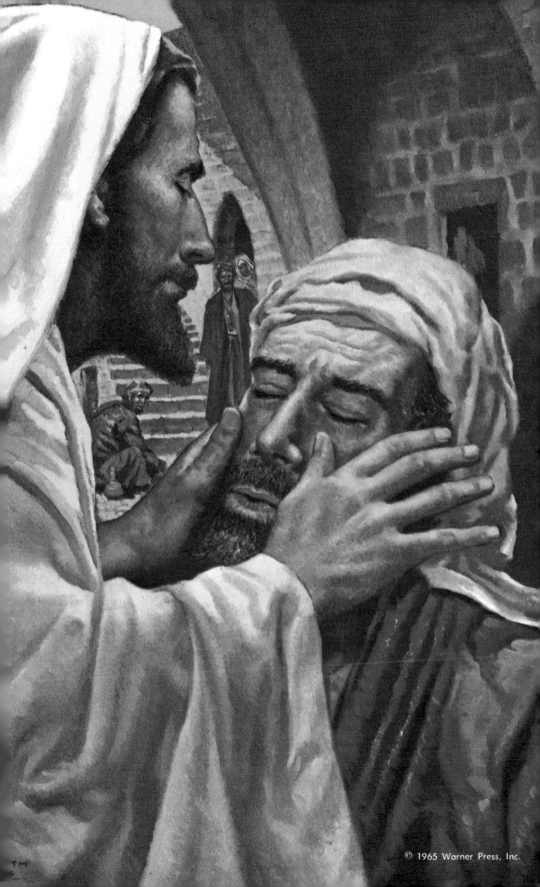

the blind man's eyes. They gathered around him and asked, "What did Jesus do to you? How did he open your eyes?"

The man told how Jesus mixed a little clay, rubbed it on his eyes, and sent him to wash in the pool of Siloam. "When I did as he commanded, I could see," he said joyfully.

"Where is this Jesus now?" the people asked. But the man did not know.

The neighbors took the man who had been blind to the Pharisees. There the rulers questioned him. Finally they said of Jesus, "This man is not of God because he does not keep the Sabbath."

Others standing by said, "How could a sinner do such miracles?"

And the people were divided. Some thought Jesus had the power of God. Others thought he deceived those who believed on him.

Turning to the man who had been healed, the Pharisees asked, "What do you say of the one who opened your eyes?"

The man replied, "I believe he is a prophet."

Jesus' enemies were much worked up over this miracle. They tried to find some way to prove it was not true. Perhaps the man had only pretended to be blind. The rulers called his parents and questioned them.

The parents were afraid. The rulers had already agreed that any one who confessed Jesus as the Christ would be turned out of the synagogue. When asked to identify their son and tell how he was made to see, they answered, "We do not know how he was made to see or who opened his eyes. He is old enough. Ask him. He will speak for himself."

Jesus' enemies grew angry. Again they asked the man who had been blind, "What did Jesus do to you? How did he open your eyes?"

He said, "I told you once, and you would not listen. If I tell you again, will you also be his disciples?"

Scornfully they said, "We are Moses' disciples, for we know God spoke to Moses. As for this fellow we do not know where he came from."

Now the man Jesus had healed said boldly, "It is strange that you do not know where Jesus came from, since he opened my blinded eyes. If any man worships God and does his will, God hears that man.

Since the world began, no one has opened the eyes of one who was born blind. If Jesus were not of God, he could do nothing."

The rulers were angry when they heard this. Because the man had dared to try to teach them, they threw him out of the synagogue. No longer would he be welcome to worship there.

When Jesus heard what had happened, he went to find the man. Jesus asked, "Do you believe on the Son of God?"

The man answered, "Who is he, Lord, that I may believe?"

And Jesus said, "You have seen him with your eyes. He is speaking to you right now."

"Lord, I believe!" the man said joyfully.

Little Children are Brought to Jesus

Matthew 19:13-15; Mark 10:13-16

While Jesus was teaching the people, mothers brought their little children. These mothers wanted Jesus to put his hands on the children and pray for them.

When the disciples saw the mothers and children, they did not like it. Because they thought Jesus was too busy to be bothered with little children, they called the mothers aside and said, "You should not trouble the Master with your children. He has more important work to do."

How disappointed the mothers and children were! They wanted to see Jesus and talk to him. Perhaps some had come a long way.

Just then Jesus saw the mothers and children. He called the children to him. Jesus felt sorry for what the disciples had done. Looking at them he said, "Do not forbid the little children to come to me, for of such is the kingdom of God. Whoever of you does not receive the kingdom of God just like a little child can never enter into it." And he took the little ones in his arms to love them.

Jesus knew that children would gladly believe him and that many times they would lead older people to believe in him too. He knew their hearts were tender and quick to respond to his love. Older people were more ready to doubt and to question whether or not he was the Christ.

The Rich Young Ruler

Matthew 19:16-30; Mark 10:17-31

One day a young man came running to meet Jesus. This rich young man wore expensive clothing. Kneeling down in the dust before Jesus, he said, "Good Master, what good thing shall I do that I may have eternal life?"

"Why do you call me good?" asked Jesus. "There is none good but God. You know the commandments—'Do not kill'; 'Do not steal'; 'Do not speak falsely'; 'Honor your father and your mother.'"

"Yes, I know the commandments of Moses," answered the young man, "and I have kept them from childhood. But I seem to lack something yet. O Master, tell me what it is!"

Jesus looked into the young man's face and loved him. How Jesus longed to help him! Jesus said, "You lack one thing. If you would be perfectly happy, go home and sell all you have and give your riches to the poor. Then you will have riches in heaven. Afterwards you may come back and be my disciple."

What a change came over the young man's face when he heard these words! With bowed head he walked slowly away, for he loved his riches.

Jesus watched him go away. Turning to the disciples he said, "How hard it is for rich men to enter the kingdom of God!" The young man loved his riches more than he loved God. He could not be happy, for his heart was not right with God. Always he would feel something was lacking, something clouding his hope of life in heaven. But he turned away from Jesus, choosing rather to be rich in this world than to be a disciple of the Lord.

Seventy Other Disciples Sent Out

Luke 10:1-24

Jesus knew he did not have much longer to preach. Soon he must lay down his life. Many people still needed to hear the gospel and be healed. To do this work Jesus chose seventy other men who had followed him and knew his teachings. He gave them power to

The rich young man turns and walks slowly away from Jesus.

KENNETH
INGLES

heal the sick. Then he sent them out, two by two, to preach in the cities and villages east of the Jordan River.

Before they left Jesus told them not to take any money or any extra clothing. He said their needs would be taken care of. They were to eat whatever was served in the home where they stayed. Then he said, "Whatever city you enter, heal the sick that are there and tell them, 'The kingdom of God is come near to you.' "

Just as the twelve disciples had done, so these seventy went forth to heal the sick and tell people of the kingdom of heaven. When their mission was over, they hurried back to tell Jesus of their success. They rejoiced because they had been able to heal the sick.

Jesus said, "Do not rejoice in this, but rather be glad that your names are written in heaven." And he gave thanks for the work that was done. Jesus prayed, "I thank you, O Father, Lord of heaven and earth."

Turning to his disciples Jesus told them, "Blessed are the eyes that see the things you see. I tell you that many prophets and kings wanted to see the things you see, but they did not see them. They wanted to hear the words you hear, but they did not hear them."

And Jesus rejoiced that his followers had preached the good news abroad.

The Good Samaritan

Luke 10:25-37

A lawyer came to Jesus and asked a question to trick him. He said, "Master, what shall I do to have eternal life?"

Jesus understood how well this man knew the Law of Moses. Instead of answering the question, he asked the lawyer, "What is written in the Law of Moses? Do you not know its teachings?"

The lawyer replied, "Moses wrote that we should love the Lord our God with all our heart, and with all our soul, and with all our strength, and with all our mind. And he wrote that we should love our neighbors as ourselves."

"You have answered right," Jesus said. "Do this and you shall have life in heaven."

But the lawyer had another question. He asked, "Who is my neighbor?"

To answer him Jesus told the story about the Good Samar'itan. This is the story:

"One day a man traveled the road from Jerusalem to Jericho. On the way robbers stopped him. They took his money, tore off his clothes, beat him, and left him half dead by the roadside.

"Soon a priest came along. He saw the injured man lying there, but he did not stop to help. He did not even say a kind word to the poor man.

Next a Levite came by. He, too, saw the wounded man lying by the road, but he did not give him a second look. He hurried on, leaving the poor man to die.

"Perhaps the man would have died if a kindhearted Samaritan had not come along. The Samaritan saw the suffering man lying there. At once he stopped his mule, climbed down, and bent over the stranger. The wounded man was a Jew. Even though the Jews were not friendly to his people the Samaritan felt he must help this Jew who was in great trouble.

"First he poured oil on the man's wounds and bandaged them. Then lifting the man to his mule, the Samaritan took him to an inn. Here he cared for the wounded man.

"On the next day the Samaritan had to continue his journey. To the innkeeper he gave money and explained, 'Take care of this man until he is well. If you need more money, I will pay it when I come back.'

"Now," asked Jesus, "which of these three men was a neighbor to the one who was attacked by robbers?"

"The man who treated him kindly," answered the lawyer.

And Jesus said, "Go, and do the same."

Lazarus Is Raised from the Dead

John 11:1-54

Laz'arus was a Jew who lived in the village of Bethany with his two sisters, Mary and Martha. Since their home was near Jerusalem, Jesus often stopped to visit them on his way to attend the feasts at the temple. Always Mary, Martha, and Lazarus welcomed him. They loved him dearly and believed he was the Christ.

One day while Jesus taught the people in the country east of the Jordan, a messenger came from Bethany. Mary and Martha had sent the messenger to tell Jesus, "Lord, the one you love is sick." The anxious sisters thought Jesus would come at once and heal their brother. They knew his great power. How much they needed him now!

But Jesus did not go at once. He explained to his disciples, "Lazarus' sickness is for the glory of God."

The sisters were greatly disappointed when the messenger returned without Jesus! They watched their brother grow weaker and weaker. Then he died. They were grief-stricken. Why hadn't Jesus come?

Still they hoped he would come, for he had raised the dead to life. The day passed, but Jesus did not arrive. At last the neighbors and friends came to help wrap Lazarus' body for burial. They carried him to a burial cave.

Mary and Martha followed, weeping bitterly. They saw Lazarus laid in the cave and watched the great stone rolled over the opening. Still Jesus had not come.

Two days after receiving the message from Mary and Martha, Jesus said to his disciples, "Let us go back to Judea again."

The disciples did not like the idea. They answered, "Master, when you were there before some of the people tried to stone you. Why go back?"

"Our friend Lazarus sleeps," Jesus told them. "I go to awaken him." At first the disciples thought Lazarus must be getting better. Then Jesus told them that Lazarus was dead. He said, "For your sakes I am glad I was not there so you may believe."

Lazarus had been dead four days. The sisters thought it would be too late for Jesus to help them now even if he did come. Friends

They are astonished to see
Lazarus alive again.

came from Jerusalem to comfort the sisters, but it was Jesus they wanted most.

At last word came that Jesus and his disciples were nearing the village. Martha ran to meet him. "Lord," she cried, "if only you had been here, my brother would not have died!"

To comfort her, Jesus said, "Your brother will rise again."

"I know he will be resurrected in the last day," she answered.

That was not what Jesus meant. He explained, "I am the resurrection and the life. He that believes in me, though he dies, yet shall he live. And those who live and believe in me shall never die. Do you believe this?" he asked.

Martha answered, "Yes, Lord, I believe you are the Christ, the Son of God."

But Martha did not really understand what Jesus meant. She left him and hurried to call her sister Mary. "The Master wants to see you, Mary," she said.

Mary hurried to meet Jesus and found him resting by the road-side. Falling at his feet she sobbed, "Lord, if you had been here my brother would not have died!"

The Jews who had come from Jerusalem to comfort the sisters saw Mary leave the house in a great hurry. They thought she was going to Lazarus' grave, so they followed. When they saw her fall weeping at Jesus' feet, they wept aloud.

"Where have you laid Lazarus' body?" Jesus asked.

They took him to the cave. Jesus wept in sympathy when he looked at the sisters and their sorrowing friends.

The Jews whispered, "See how much he loved Lazarus! Surely this man who opened blind eyes could have healed Lazarus."

While they talked, Jesus commanded that someone roll the stone away from the front of the cave.

Martha exclaimed, "Lord, he has been dead four days. By this time his body is decaying!"

Jesus answered, "Did I not tell you that you would see the glory of God if you believed?"

The stone was rolled away. While the people watched, Jesus lifted his eyes to heaven and said, "Father, I thank you that you have heard me. And I know that you hear me always. I say this so the people who are here may believe you have sent me." Then Jesus looked into the door of the cave and cried with a loud voice, "Lazarus, come out!"

Speechless, the people watched. How astonished they were to see Lazarus get up and come out!

Jesus said, "Take off the burial clothes and let him go." And Lazarus went home with his sisters and Jesus.

The Jews who had seen this miracle believed that Jesus was the Christ. Soon the scribes and Pharisees and chief priests heard what had happened at Bethany. How excited they were! "What shall we do?" they asked. "If we let him go on, soon all men will believe in him. Then the Romans will take away our nation."

From that time Jesus' enemies planned how they would capture and kill him.

A Sick Man Is Healed

Luke 14:1-6

Jesus knew his enemies were plotting against him in Jerusalem. For that reason he and his disciples returned to the country near the Jordan River. Here Jesus preached and healed all the sick who were brought to him.

One Sabbath a Pharisee who lived near by invited Jesus to his house for dinner. Jesus accepted. Many people gathered at the Pharisee's house. Among the guests were Pharisees and lawyers. Others had come without being invited. These stood around the dining hall and watched while the guests ate.

One man who looked on had a sickness called dropsy. He must have heard that Jesus would be here. The man wanted very much to be healed.

When Jesus saw the sick man, he felt sorry for him. Jesus, too, wanted the man to be well again. Turning to the Pharisees and lawyers, he asked, "Is it lawful to heal on the Sabbath?"

The men refused to answer. Then Jesus healed the man and sent him away. Jesus said, "If one of your animals should fall into a pit on the Sabbath, not one of you would wait until after the Sabbath to pull him out."

87

Because the Pharisees and the lawyers understood that Jesus was teaching them to be merciful to people as well as to animals, they could not think of anything to say to him. Perhaps they felt ashamed.

The Parable of the Supper

Luke 14:7-24

After they had finished dinner at the Pharisee's house, Jesus began to teach. He had noticed that when the guests had arrived, each one tried to get the best place for himself. Jesus wanted them to think more of others than of themselves.

He said, "When you are invited to a wedding, do not choose the most honored place for yourself. A person more important than you may come. Then you will be asked to give your place to him, and you will be embarrassed. Instead, if you take the lowest place, you may be called up higher. Your friends will honor you."

Then Jesus turned to the Pharisee who had given the dinner and said, "When you prepare a feast, do not invite your friends and relatives and rich neighbors. They will return your invitation. If you want to be rewarded in heaven, invite the poor and the crippled and the blind to your feasts. Such people cannot repay you, and God will bless you for your kindness."

One of the guests who listened to these words said, "Blessed is he who will eat bread in the kingdom of God."

To all those present Jesus told a story about the kingdom of God. He said:

"A certain man gave a great supper and invited many guests. When everything was ready, he sent his servant to bring the guests. But each one made an excuse for not attending.

"The first man said, 'I have just bought a piece of ground, and I must go to see it. Please excuse me this time.'

"Another man said, 'I have just bought five yoke of oxen and I want to try them out. I'd like to be excused this time.'

"A third said, 'I have just been married, and I want to stay home with my wife. Won't you please excuse me?'

"Everywhere the servant went the guests asked to be excused. The

88

master was very angry when the servant returned alone. He ordered, 'Go quickly into the streets and lanes of the city. Bring the poor, the crippled, the old, and the blind.'

"The servant obeyed, but still there was room for more. The master said, 'Go out into the country places and bring others.' And the house was filled with hungry people who enjoyed the good food."

A Crippled Woman Is Healed

Luke 13:11-17

Jesus went to teach in the cities and villages where the Seventy had preached and healed. On the Sabbath he went to a synagogue to worship. There he saw a woman who was badly bent over. For eighteen years she had not been able to straighten her back or shoulders. Jesus knew how hard it must be for the woman to get around. Calling her to him, he said, "Woman, you are no longer crippled." He put his hands on her bent back, and she was able to stand straight again.

The woman was very happy, and she praised God that she was well.

The ruler of the synagogue was angry that Jesus had healed on the Sabbath. He said, "There are six days in the week for men to work. Let the sick be healed on those days and not on the Sabbath."

But Jesus replied, "You are only pretending to keep the Law and please God. Do you untie your animals and lead them to water on the Sabbath? Then why should not this poor woman be loosed on the Sabbath from the thing that has crippled her for eighteen years?"

These words made Jesus' enemies feel ashamed. The other people praised God because they had seen his wonderful works.

Jesus Answers the Pharisees

Luke 13:31-35; 15:1-10

One day some Pharisees came to Jesus and said, "Leave here quickly, for Herod wants to kill you." They hoped Jesus would be frightened and run away. Then they would be rid of him.

Jesus was not afraid of Herod. He knew his greatest enemies were among the rulers of the Jews. They hated him because he reminded them of their sins and because he taught the poor people.

To the Pharisees Jesus said, "Go to Herod and tell him I am at work healing the sick today and tomorrow, and on the third day I shall be made perfect. I must go on my way today, tomorrow, and even the following day. It cannot be that a prophet should die outside Jerusalem." Jesus remembered how the Jews had killed God's prophets in other days. It was the Jewish leaders and not Herod who would condemn him to death.

Many tax collectors and sinners followed Jesus and listened to his words. That was why the Pharisees and scribes found fault with him. They said, "This man receives sinners and even eats with them."

Jesus knew what they were doing, so he spoke to the people in parables or stories. He saw many women in the crowd so he told a story they would understand well.

"What woman," he asked, "who has ten pieces of silver and loses one does not do everything she can to find it? She lights a candle and looks for it. Then she sweeps the house and looks everywhere. When she finds it she calls to her neighbors and friends, 'Rejoice with me, for I have found the money I lost.'

"In the same way," said Jesus, "there is rejoicing in heaven when one lost sinner comes to God."

The Prodigal Son

Luke 15:11-32

As the people listened eagerly, Jesus told them this story:

"A certain man had two sons. The younger said, 'Father give me my share of the money that I am to have when you die.'

90

"So the father divided his wealth between his two sons. The younger packed his things and went on a long trip. He spent his money freely. He wasted most of it in having a good time. At first there were many friends to enjoy the money with him. When the money was all spent, the friends were gone too.

"About this time there was a famine in the land, and the young man became hungry. He got a job tending hogs for a farmer. Even then the young man did not have enough to eat. He even wished someone would give him some of the food that was thrown to the hogs.

"How miserable the young man was! Finally he said to himself, 'My father has many servants who have plenty to eat, and here I am starving. I will go back to my father and tell him how I have sinned. I will tell him that I'm not worthy to be his son, and I would like to be one of his servants.' And the young man started home.

"The father missed his younger son. He worried about his boy. Every day he longed for his son to come home. Every day he watched for him.

"One day in the distance the father saw a man coming. As the man got nearer, the father could see that he was ragged. Soon the father recognized the young man as his son. Running to meet him the father threw his arms around the boy.

" 'Father,' the son said, 'I have sinned against heaven and against you. I am no longer worthy to be your son. . . .'

"Before the son could finish, the father ordered the servants, 'Bring the best robe and put it on him. Put a ring on his finger and shoes on his feet. Prepare a feast. Let us eat and rejoice, for the son who I thought was dead is alive. He was lost, but now he is found.' All the household rejoiced.

"While this was happening, the older son was working in the field. When he returned to the house and heard all the excitement, he asked, 'What has happened?'

"The servants said, 'Your brother has come back. Your father is giving a dinner because the boy has returned safe and sound.'

"The older brother was not happy. Indeed, he was angry. He would not even go into the house. The father came out and talked to his older son. The selfish older son could think only of himself. He said,

'I have served you faithfully all these years, but you do not rejoice over me. Now when my brother comes back after spending all his money on wild living, you celebrate.'

"At once the father knew his older son was jealous. He said, 'Son, you have always been with me. Everything I have is yours. I thought your brother was dead, but he is alive. It is right to rejoice because he has come back. Though he was lost, now he is found.' "

The Rich Man and Lazarus

Luke 16:19-31

There was a certain rich man who thought only of himself. He wore expensive clothes. Every day he ate the best kind of food. His many servants were quick to do his bidding. He lived only to enjoy himself.

At the rich man's gate lay a beggar named Laz'arus. He was too ill to work for a living, so he asked for the crumbs that fell from the rich man's table. He felt he had a right to ask for help, since both he and the rich man were descendants of Abraham. But the rich man would not help Lazarus at all. Even the dogs seemed sorry for Lazarus, but not the rich man.

Finally Lazarus died and the angels carried him to heaven. Here he was not a beggar. He could live in peace and happiness with Abraham and other good people who had left the world.

Later the rich man died. His friends buried him in a new cave and mourned for him. The rich man was taken to a place of torment. There he lifted up his eyes. Far, far away he saw Lazarus. How happy Lazarus looked with Abraham! The rich man cried out, "Abraham, have mercy on me. Send Lazarus that he may dip the tip of his finger in water and cool my burning tongue."

Abraham answered, "Remember the good things you enjoyed in your lifetime while Lazarus had only trouble and suffering. Now he is comforted and you are tormented. I can send nothing to you because no one can pass from this place to your place of torment."

The rich man remembered his brothers who were still living on the earth. He did not want them to come to this place. He said,

93

The father runs to throw
his arms around his son.

"Please send Lazarus back to my father's house. He must warn my five brothers about this dreadful place."

Abraham answered, "They have the words of Moses and the prophets. Let them obey those words."

The rich man knew his brothers would never do that. He pleaded, "No, but if someone were to be sent from the dead, they would repent."

Finally Abraham said, "If they will not pay any attention to the words in God's book, they would not pay any attention to one who rose from the dead."

The Unjust Judge

Luke 18:1-8

God does not always answer prayer right away. Sometimes he wants to make sure people are really in earnest about what they pray for. He lets them come to him again and again before he gives the things they ask. To teach men to keep on praying until their prayers are answered, Jesus told the story of the unjust judge.

A poor widow had been wronged by an emeny. She could not punish her enemy or get back what he had taken, so she went to the city judge for help.

The judge was not a good man. He was not interested in helping the widow. At first he did not even pay any attention to her. But the woman kept coming to see him about her troubles.

Finally he got tired of her coming. He said to himself, "Even though I am not a good man, I will do what this widow wants so she will stop bothering me."

Then Jesus said, "Learn a lesson from this unjust judge. He did what the woman wanted because she came to him often. Shall God not grant the wishes of those who call on him day and night?"

The Pharisee and the Publican

Luke 18:9-14

In the crowd were people who were proud of their righteousness. They despised those who they thought were sinners. To teach them a lesson Jesus told this story:

"Two men went up to the temple to pray. One was a Pharisee and the other a tax collector.

"The Pharisee stood and prayed loudly for all to hear, 'God, I thank you that I am not like other men, unrighteous, unjust, unfair in business dealings, or even like this tax collector. I fast twice a week. I give a tenth of all I own.'

"But the tax collector stood by himself. He would not even lift his eyes toward heaven when he prayed. Bowing his head, he beat his breast and said, 'God, be merciful to me a sinner!' "

And Jesus said, "I tell you, this tax collector, and not the proud Pharisee, went home with God's blessing. For whoever lifts himself up in his own sight is not pleasing to God, but whoever humbles himself shall be lifted up."

James and John Want to Be Honored

Matthew 20:17-28; Mark 10:32-45; Luke 18:31-34

It was time again for the Passover Feast at Jerusalem. Jesus knew this would be the last one he would attend. He wanted to prepare his disciples for the things that would happen. He said, "We go up to Jerusalem. The Son of man will be betrayed into the hands of the chief priests and scribes. They will condemn him to death. They will take him to the Gentiles. The Gentiles will mock, beat, and crucify him. On the third day he will rise again."

But the disciples did not understand. They still believed he would become the earthly king of the Jews.

Then the mother of James and John came to him with her two sons. She knelt before him and asked a favor.

"What do you want?" Jesus asked her.

95

She said, "Let one of my sons sit on your right hand and the other on the left in your kingdom."

Jesus told James and John, "You don't know what you ask for. Can you drink from the cup that I drink of and be baptized with the baptism that I am baptized with?"

"We are able," they answered.

Jesus said, "That is true, but it is not mine to give the places on my right hand and on my left. They shall be given to those for whom my Father has prepared them."

When the other disciples found out what James and John had wanted, they were angry. Why should James and John ask to be honored above them?

Jesus called his disciples and told them, "You know the rulers of the Gentiles have great authority. It shall not be the same among you. Whoever wants to be great among you, let him be your minister. Whoever wants to be chief among you, let him be your servant. Even the Son of man did not come to be ministered unto, but to minister and to give his life a ransom for many."

As Jesus and his disciples left Jericho a great crowd followed.

Blind Bartimeus

Matthew 20:29-34; Mark 10:46-52; Luke 18:35-43

Many people were on their way to Jerusalem for the Passover. A crowd traveled with Jesus and his disciples. Many of them had heard Jesus teach and had seen him heal the sick. The news of Jesus' coming was told throughout the country. Some stood by the roadside just to see him go by.

Outside the city of Jericho sat Bartime'us, begging from the people who passed. He heard the sound of many footsteps and wondered why such a crowd was passing. Someone told him, "Jesus of Nazareth is going by."

Bartimeus had heard of Jesus. Probably someone had told him how Jesus had healed the man who had been blind since birth. How much Bartimeus, too, wanted to receive his sight. He got up from his seat by the roadside and called out loudly, "Jesus, Son of David, have mercy on me."

Some who stood near Bartimeus tried to quiet him. Instead he called out the more loudly, "Jesus, Son of David, have mercy on me."

Jesus stood still. He commanded that the blind man be brought to him. Those who went to get the blind man told him, "Be of good comfort. Come, he calls for you."

How glad Bartimeus was! He threw off his cloak and went to Jesus.

Jesus asked, "What do you want me to do for you?"

"Lord, give me my sight," Bartimeus said.

Jesus answered, "Go your way. Your faith has made you well."

At once the blind eyes opened and Bartimeus could see as well as those who had never been blind. He followed Jesus, glorifying God.

When the people saw what had happened, they too praised God.

Zaccheus Climbs a Tree

Luke 19:1-10

In Jericho lived a rich man named Zacche'us, who was the head tax collector. When news came that Jesus was passing through Jericho on his way to Jerusalem, Zaccheus wanted more than anything else to see this wonderful man.

Zaccheus stood with the crowd gathered beside the road, but he could see nothing. He was too short to see over the heads of the people. Down the road he ran and climbed into a sycamore tree. Now he could surely see Jesus.

Soon travelers going to Jerusalem came along the road. The people of Jericho watched eagerly to catch a glimpse of Jesus. On the travelers walked until they came to the sycamore tree. Here Jesus and his disciples stood still. Jesus looked up and saw Zaccheus.

"Zaccheus," called Jesus, "come down at once, for today I must stop at your house."

How surprised Zaccheus was! Now he could take Jesus home and talk with him.

Joyfully Zaccheus led the way. As they went, others followed.

97

Some found fault because Jesus was stopping in the home of a tax collector whom they called a sinful man. The Pharisees would not enter such a house. They hated sinners.

Zaccheus' heart was changed by Jesus' kind words. He told Jesus, "Behold, Lord, I will give half of my goods to the poor. And if I have taken more from any man than I should, I will give back four times as much as I took."

Jesus was glad to hear Zaccheus say that. Jesus answered, "Today salvation is come to your house, for the Son of man is come to seek and to save those who are lost."

The Parable of the Pounds

Luke 19:11-27

Because many people were listening, Jesus told a parable or story sermon. He knew the people were expecting the kingdom of heaven to be set up soon like an earthly kingdom. He hoped this story would help them understand what the kingdom of heaven is like. Jesus said:

"A certain nobleman went to a far country to receive a kingdom. Before leaving home he gave a sum of money, called a pound, to each of his ten servants. They were to use the money until his return.

"When the nobleman came back, he called the ten servants and asked how they had used the money.

"The first servant brought the money and said, 'I traded with the pound you gave me, and I have gained ten pounds.' The nobleman was pleased and said, 'Because you have done this, you are to rule ten cities in my kingdom.'

"Next came a servant who had gained five pounds by using the money wisely. To him the nobleman said, 'To you I will give the rule of five cities in my kingdom.'

"Then a third servant brought only the one pound the nobleman had given him. 'Here is your pound. I kept it wrapped in this napkin while you were away. I was afraid I might lose it, and I knew you were a harsh master.'

"The nobleman answered, 'If you knew I was a harsh master, why did you not put my money into a bank that I might have it and its interest on my return?' He commanded those who stood by, 'Take the one pound from the unfaithful servant and give it to the one who has ten.'

"The servants asked, 'Lord, he has ten pounds; why give him more?'

"He answered, 'To every one who uses what he has, more shall be given, but he who does not use what he has shall have it taken away.' "

Mary Anoints Jesus

Matthew 26:6-13; Mark 14:3-9; John 12:1-11

"Jesus is coming! Jesus is coming!" the news spread through Bethany quickly. How glad his friends were to hear this! What could they do to welcome him and show him their love?

Simon, who had once been a leper, planned to have a supper at his house for Jesus. Martha at once busied herself helping to get the meal ready. She was very thankful to Jesus for raising her brother from the dead. Helping with this dinner was one way she could show her thanks.

Laz'arus eagerly awaited Jesus' coming too. When the people heard that Lazarus would be at this dinner, they wanted to see him. Was it really true that he had been raised from the dead? What did he look like? They would see for themselves. Although they were not invited they would go and stand around the room to watch.

Mary, too, wanted to see Jesus again. No women were invited to eat this dinner with Jesus and his disciples, but that would not keep Mary from seeing him. She must find some way to show him her love.

At last Jesus and his disciples arrived. Simon welcomed them to his home. The guests were brought into the dining hall and the food was served. Curious onlookers crowded in.

While the guests ate, Mary brought a container of expensive perfume. It had taken a whole year's wages to buy it, but she wanted to give Jesus her very best. Mary made her way to the couch where Jesus reclined. She poured the rare perfume on his head and feet. Then she knelt and wiped his feet with her hair.

As soon as the container was broken, the scent of sweet perfume filled the air. People knew at once that this perfume was expensive. The disciples began to whisper among themselves, "Why has she done this?"

Judas Iscariot, who was treasurer for the disciples, said, "Why wasn't this perfume sold and the money given to the poor?"

Jesus knew what his disciples thought. He told them, "Let this woman alone. Why should you trouble her? She has done a good work. She has anointed my body for burial. You will always have the poor with you, but I shall not be with you much longer. By this anointing, Mary has shown her love for me. I tell you, wherever the gospel is preached throughout the world, it will be told that Mary did this for her Lord."

Judas Iscariot did not like Jesus' words, for he loved money. He hoped to be a rich ruler in the kingdom he expected Jesus to set up. After the supper was over Judas went to Jerusalem to see the chief priests and scribes. He would turn Jesus over to them.

For many days Jesus' enemies had planned how they might capture the Master. After Lazarus had been raised from the dead, they were all the more eager to get rid of Jesus because he had gained many new followers.

Jesus Rides into Jerusalem as King

Matthew 21:1-11; Mark 11:1-11; Luke 19:29-40; John 12:12-19

All Jerusalem was excited. People flocked out the city gate and hurried along the road to Mount Olivet. Many of them had come to Jerusalem for the Passover. They wanted to meet Jesus because they had heard so much about him.

As Jesus and his disciples came near to Jerusalem, he said to two of them, "Go to the village near by. As you enter the village, you will see a colt that has never been ridden. Untie him and bring him to me. If anyone asks, 'Why do you do this?' say, 'The Lord has need of him.' "

The two disciples went to the village, found the colt, and untied it. Some asked, "Why are you untying that colt?" When they heard that Jesus needed the colt they let it go.

100

Two disciples find a
colt for Jesus to ride.

The disciples brought the colt to Jesus and spread their coats on its back. Then Jesus sat on the colt. Many people spread their clothes along the road for Jesus to ride over. Others waved palm branches. They shouted, "Blessed is the King who is coming in the name of the Lord! Peace in heaven and glory in the highest!" All along the way people were rejoicing and praising God.

In the crowd were Pharisees who had come to find fault. They said to Jesus, "Make the people stop shouting."

Jesus answered, "If they should be still, the stones would immediately cry out."

As Jesus rode up Mount Mori'ah to the temple, the people shouted, "Hosanna to the Son of David!"

The city people hurried into the streets to ask, "Who is this?"

The crowd answered, "This is Jesus, the prophet from Nazareth of Galilee."

Jesus Teaches in the Temple

Matthew 21:12-27; Mark 11:12-33; Luke 19:41–20:17

Early the next morning Jesus and his disciples left Bethany where they had spent each night during the feast. They were on their way to the temple at Jerusalem. As they walked along Jesus became hungry. By the roadside he saw a fig tree. When he looked for figs on its branches, there were none. As he walked away, he said, "Never again will anyone eat fruit from this tree."

When they reached Jerusalem, Jesus and his disciples went to the temple. Here Jesus saw men buying and selling animals for sacrifices. Others were changing money into temple coins. Jesus knew they cheated the people. Once before he had driven these men out of the temple.

Again he drove them out. "In the Scriptures it is written, 'My house shall be called a house of prayer,'" Jesus said, "but you have made it a den of thieves."

When word spread through the city that Jesus was at the temple, the blind and lame were brought to him. Jesus healed them all. While the chief priests and scribes watched him do this, little children came singing, "Hosanna to the Son of David," as they gathered around Jesus.

In anger the chief priests and scribes asked him, "Do you hear what these children are saying?"

"Yes, I hear them," Jesus said. "Have you not read these words in the Scriptures, 'Out of the mouths of little children comes perfect praise'?"

How angry the chief priests and scribes were! They wanted all the more to get rid of Jesus, but they could find no way. They were afraid to do anything here, for all the people listened eagerly to his every word.

In the evening Jesus and his disciples walked back to Bethany to stay with their friends. When they returned to Jerusalem the next morning, they passed the fig tree they had seen the day before. Its leaves were all withered, dry and dead. How could this happen in one day?

Jesus told his disciples, "Have faith in God. If you have faith to believe that God hears your prayers, you will do greater things than this. When you ask anything of God in prayer and believe in your hearts that he hears you, it will be given you."

As they entered the temple this time, many people were already waiting to hear Jesus teach. Of course the chief priests and scribes were there too. Since they did not want Jesus to teach the people, they tried to start an argument. "By what authority do you teach and work miracles? Who gave you this authority?" they demanded.

Jesus said, "I will answer your question if you will first answer mine. Was the baptism of John from heaven or of men?"

The chief priests and scribes did not know what to say. They talked among themselves. "If we say John's baptism was from heaven, he will ask us why we didn't believe that John was God's prophet. We dare not say his baptism was of men, for all these people would rise up against us."

Because they were afraid to answer Jesus' question, they said, "We cannot tell whether John's baptism was from heaven or of men."

Then Jesus answered, "Nor will I tell you by what authority I do these things or who gave me this authority."

The Parable of the Two Sons

Matthew 21:28-32

Jesus told the people this story: "A certain man had two sons. He went to his older son and said, 'Son, go and work in my vineyard today.'

"The boy answered his father roughly, 'I will not go.' Afterwards he was sorry he had answered his father that way. Then he went and did what his father had asked.

"Of the second son the father made the same request. The young man replied, 'I go, sir.' But the second son did not keep his promise.

"Now," Jesus asked, "which of the two obeyed his father?"

"The first son," the people answered.

Jesus explained, "Truly, I tell you that sinners will enter the kingdom of God before you who pretend to be righteous. John preached to you, but you did not believe him. The sinners believed his message. Even though you saw it, you did not repent and believe." Jesus wanted them to understand that God does not want promises but right living.

The Parable of the Wicked Farmers

Matthew 21:33-46; Mark 12:1-12; Luke 20:9-19

"Listen to another story," Jesus said. "There was a man who planted a vineyard and fenced it in. After digging a winepress and building a watchtower, he hired farmers to take care of his vineyard while he was in another country.

"When harvesttime came, the owner sent servants to the farmers to get some of the fruit. The farmers treated the servants roughly. They beat the first one and sent him away without any fruit. They threw stones at the second one and injured him. They even killed the third servant.

"Later the owner sent other servants, and the same thing happened. At last the owner decided, 'I will send my son. They will respect him.'

"From the watchtower the farmers saw the son coming. They said

105

Jesus asked, "Which of the two sons obeyed his father?"

to each other, 'The owner has sent his son. This vineyard will belong to him when his father dies. Let us kill the son and take this vineyard for our own.' And that is what they did."

Then Jesus asked, "When the owner returns, what will he do to those men?"

The people answered, "He will make them pay with their lives. Then he will hire better men to care for his vineyard. The new men will give him a share of the fruit that grows."

Jesus looked boldly at his enemies who were standing in the crowd. He told them, "The kingdom of God will be taken from you and given to another people who will show by their lives that they are the children of God."

The chief priests and scribes knew Jesus had accused them in the story he told. In their anger they would have seized him, but they were afraid of the crowd, for the people believed that Jesus was a prophet.

The Parable of the Wedding Feast

Matthew 22:1-14

To help the people understand what the kingdom of heaven is like, Jesus told them this story:

"A king gave a feast when his son was married. Many guests from a near-by city were invited. When everything was ready, the guests did not arrive.

"The king sent his servants to remind the people of the wedding feast. Still they would not come. They made fun of it and went on with their work. Some even mistreated and killed the king's servants.

"When the king heard what had happened, he was angry. He called out his army and ordered them to burn the city and destroy those who had killed his servants.

"Then he said to his servants, 'The wedding feast is ready, but those that were invited are not worthy to come. Go into the highways and invite everyone to the marriage.'

"The servants obeyed. Among these guests were the rich and the poor, the good and the bad. To each one the king gave a special robe to wear for the wedding.

"When the king came to welcome these guests, he saw one man dressed in dirty rags. This man had refused to put on the wedding robe the king had provided. The king asked, 'Friend, why did you not put on the wedding garment I gave you?'

"The man hung his head, for he had no excuse. Angrily the king told his servants, 'Tie him up hand and foot and take him away.'"

Jesus wanted to help people understand that many who were counting on entering heaven because of good religious acts alone would be disappointed. The gates would be open only to those who truly repented of their sins.

Jesus' Enemies Come with Questions

Matthew 22:15–23:39; Mark 12:13-40; Luke 20:20-47

Jesus' enemies decided that the only way they could keep him from teaching was to interrupt him with many questions. First they sent Pharisees to ask if it was right to pay taxes to Caesar, the Roman ruler.

The Jews hated to pay these taxes. Jesus' enemies knew the people would no longer want to make Jesus their king if he said it was right for them to pay taxes. But if Jesus said it was wrong to pay taxes, his enemies would report him to the Roman government. Then the Romans would punish him.

When the Pharisees came to Jesus, they said, "Master, we know you are true. You teach God's way without caring whether people like what you say or not." The Pharisees did not believe this, but they wanted to flatter Jesus. Then they added, "Tell us what you think. Is it right or wrong to pay tax money to Caesar?"

The Pharisees had thought Jesus would answer either yes or no, but they were mistaken. Jesus knew the evil in their hearts. He paid no attention to their flattery. "Why do you tempt me, you hypocrites?" he asked. "Show me the money."

They brought him a penny. Jesus looked at the coin on both sides. "Whose likeness is this on the coin? Whose name is written here?"

The men explained that Caesar's name and picture were on the coin. "Then," said Jesus, "give to Caesar the things that belong to him, and give to God the things that belong to God."

How surprised the men were at his answer! Again they had failed to trick Jesus. Now they still had no reason to accuse him. Other enemies brought hard questions, and Jesus answered them all.

One who came to question Jesus was a lawyer. He asked, "Which is the greatest commandment of the Law?"

Jesus answered, " 'Thou shalt love the Lord thy God with all thy heart, and with all thy soul, and with all thy mind, and with all thy strength'; this is the first commandment. And the second greatest is this: 'Thou shalt love thy neighbor as thyself.' No other commandments are so important as these."

The lawyer looked at Jesus and said, "Master, that is true. There is one God and no other but him. To love him with all one's heart, understanding, soul, and strength while one loves his neighbor as himself is surely more pleasing to God than burnt offerings and sacrifices."

Jesus was pleased to hear the lawyer say this. Jesus told the man kindly, "You are not far from the kingdom of God."

After that no one dared ask Jesus any question.

Jesus' Last Hours in the Temple

Mark 12:41-44; Luke 21:1-4; John 12:20-36

During the feast the Greeks who had come to worship told Philip, "Sir, we would like to see Jesus." Because they were not Jews they could not enter the part of the temple where Jesus was teaching. They had to stay in the outside court, called the Court of the Gentiles.

Philip told Andrew that men from Greece wanted to see Jesus. Together they went to tell Jesus.

Jesus told Philip and Andrew, "The hour is come that the Son of man should be glorified." The disciples did not understand what Jesus meant, for he was speaking of his death.

Jesus hated the thought of pain just as anyone does. He felt

108

The poor widow puts two small
coins in the Temple treasury.

troubled that his time was so short. Prayerfully he said, "Father, save me from this hour." Remembering that his work would not be finished if he did not die for sinners, he added, "Father, glorify thy name."

At that instant a voice from heaven answered, "I have glorified it, and I will glorify it again."

The people who stood near by heard the voice, but they could not understand the words. Some said, "It is thundering." Others replied, "An angel spoke to him."

When Jesus heard the voice from heaven, he felt strengthened. He found a place to sit down near the temple treasury. Here were the money boxes where the people gave their offerings. Jesus saw rich men give large offerings. Also he saw a poor widow stop to put in two small coins. Together these coins were worth less than a penny.

Turning to his disciples, Jesus said, "Truly, I tell you this poor widow has given more than anyone else. Others had plenty to give. She is poor, yet she gave all that she had."

With his disciples Jesus left the temple for the last time.

The Parable of the Ten Virgins

Matthew 25:1-13

On the Mount of Olives Jesus told his disciples another story about the kingdom of heaven. He said, "It is like ten young women, called virgins, who took their lamps and went to meet the bridegroom. Five of the young women were wise and five were foolish. All of them had been invited to the marriage of a friend.

"Together they started to meet the wedding party. Since the wedding was to take place at night, they took their lamps for light. The foolish five did not take oil for their lamps.

"The young women waited and waited. The wedding party was slow in coming. The young women became so tired that they fell asleep.

"About midnight someone called out, 'The bridegroom is coming. Go out to meet him.'

"At that the young women got up and trimmed their lamps so

they would be ready to join the procession. The foolish five discovered that their oil was gone. 'What shall we do?' they cried. Then they turned to their friends and said, 'Please give us some of your oil, for our lamps have gone out.'

" 'We cannot give you oil,' the wise young women answered. 'If we do, there will not be enough for us. Go and buy yourselves some oil.'

"The foolish young women had no choice. They went to buy oil. While they were gone, the wedding party came. The wise young women joined the party on the way to the bridegroom's house.

"When all the guests were inside, the door was shut. Now no one else was welcome. The foolish young women arrived after the door was shut. They knocked and called out, 'Open to us.' But the bridegroom would not let them in. They had come too late."

Jesus told this story to teach the disciples that they must always be ready for his coming. They would never know when he would call for them to leave this world and go to be with him. If they were not ready when he called, they too would be shut out.

Jesus Tells About the End of the World

Matthew 25:31-46

Jesus told his disciples that at the end of the world the Son of man will come in his glory with the angels. He will sit upon his throne. Before him all the nations of the earth will be gathered. Then he will divide the good from the evil. Those who have believed in him, he will place on his right. Those who have disobeyed, he will place on his left. The good and the evil will be divided just as the shepherd divides the sheep from the goats.

"Then shall the Son of man be King," said Jesus. "He will say to those on his right, 'Come, you who are blessed of my Father, and live in the kingdom which has been prepared for you. For I was hungry, and you fed me. I was thirsty, and you gave me drink. I was a stranger, and you took me in. I did not have clothes to wear, but you gave me some. I was sick, and you visited me. I was in prison and you came to see me there.'

"And the ones on the right will reply, 'Lord, when did we see you in need and do all this for you?'

"And the King will answer, 'Whenever you helped one needy person, you helped me.'

"Then the King will turn to those on his left and say, 'Depart from me, you who are cursed, into the everlasting punishment that has been prepared for the devil and his helpers. For I was hungry, and you did not feed me. I was thirsty, and you gave me nothing to drink. I was a stranger, and you would not take me in. I was without clothes, but you did not help me. I was sick, but you did not visit me. I was in prison, but you did not come to me there.'

"And the ones on the left will reply, 'Lord, when did we see you hungry, or thirsty, or without clothes, or a stranger, or sick, or in prison, and not help you?'

"And he will say to them, 'Whenever you refused to help anyone, you refused to help me.'

"And those on the right," said Jesus, "will go into life eternal, but those on the left will have everlasting punishment."

The Last Supper with the Twelve
Matthew 26:17-30; Mark 14:12-26; Luke 22:3-39; John 13

"Where shall we go to prepare the Passover meal?" the disciples asked Jesus.

Jesus told Peter and John, "Go into the city, and there you will meet a man carrying a pitcher of water; follow him. When he goes into his house, say to him, 'Where is the guest room where Jesus is to eat the Passover with his disciples?' "

The two went their way. It was as Jesus had said. The owner of the house led them to an upstairs room. Probably he knew Jesus and was glad to have him use the guest room.

When evening came Jesus and the other ten joined Peter and John. A feeling of sadness crept over them when Jesus said that this was his last supper with them.

Would Jesus really be taken away from them? It seemed impossible to think men ever could kill him. And soon they were talking

113

Jesus says, "One of you
will betray me."

about other matters at the supper table. Some wondered who would be the greatest in Jesus' kingdom. They did not understand his teachings.

Jesus knew their thoughts and wanted to teach them more about his kingdom. He got up from the table, took off his outer coat, and tied a towel around his waist. Taking a basin of water, he began to wash their feet.

The disciples looked at each other in surprise. Why should Jesus do this? They had washed their feet before coming into the upper room. Peter pulled his feet away from Jesus and exclaimed, "Lord, you shall never wash my feet!"

"If I wash you not," said Jesus, "you shall never have a part in my kingdom."

But Peter wanted a part in Jesus' kingdom! He said, "Lord, wash not only my feet, but also my hands and my head."

When the washing was over, Jesus laid aside the towel and put on his coat again. He explained, "You call me Lord, and Master, and so I am. If I, your Lord and Master, have washed your feet, you ought to wash one another's feet. For I have given you an example that you should do to each other as I have done to you. The servant is not greater than his master, and if you would be good servants you will obey my words. If you know my commands, you will be happy when you obey them."

Being troubled, Jesus said, "One of you will betray me."

How could this be? The disciples began asking, "Lord, is it I?"

Jesus said, "It is the one to whom I shall give this piece of bread when I have dipped it." Jesus gave the bread to Judas Iscariot and said, "Whatever you do, do quickly." Immediately Judas left the room and went out into the night.

The disciples did not understand. Because Judas took care of the money, they thought he was going to do something for Jesus.

After supper Jesus took bread, offered thanks, broke the bread in pieces, and gave each disciple a piece. "Take this bread and eat it, for it is my body which is broken for you." Then he took the cup. When he had given thanks he passed it to them saying, "Drink this, for it is my blood, which is shed for you. I will never again drink of the fruit of the vine with you until that day when I drink it new in the kingdom of God."

Jesus told them that he would soon die and leave them alone. They should not be afraid. "After I am risen, I will go before you into Galilee."

Peter said, "Lord, I'll never leave you!"

Jesus answered, "This night before the cock crows, you will deny me three times."

Then Jesus and his disciples sang a hymn together, left the upper room, and went to the Garden of Gethsem'ane.

Two Disciples Fail Their Lord
Matthew 26:14-16, 36-75; Mark 14:10-11, 32-72; Luke 22:1-6, 39-71; John 18:1-27

Judas Iscariot went to the chief priests and asked, "What will you give me if I turn Jesus over to you?" And they promised him thirty pieces of silver.

After leaving the upper room, Jesus and the Eleven went to the Garden of Gethsem'ane. At the entrance Jesus told eight disciples, "Stay here while I go and pray." Taking Peter, James, and John, he went into the garden to pray.

While he prayed, the disciples fell asleep.They could not understand why he was so troubled, and they did not know how to comfort him. How he longed to have them near to pray with him! Twice Jesus awakened Peter, James, and John. Then while he prayed in agony alone, God sent an angel to strengthen and comfort him.

Jesus knew he would die on the cross. He must bear the sins of the world in order to become the Savior of men. Because he had a body and mind like ours, he dreaded to suffer the pain of such a death and he dreaded to be left alone by those he loved. So he prayed, "O my Father, if it be possible, let this pass away from me. Nevertheless not my will but thine be done."

A third time Jesus roused the sleeping disciples, saying, "Rise, let us be going; my betrayer is near." They followed. At the entrance they saw men carrying torches. Judas, the untrue disciple, was with the men. Stepping forward he said, "Hail, Master!" and kissed Jesus on the cheek.

Jesus looked sadly at this disciple and asked, "Judas, do you betray the Son of man with a kiss?"

Judas had told the men he would kiss Jesus so they would know whom to take prisoner. Taking hold of Jesus roughly, the soldiers led him away.

At this Peter drew a short sword, struck one of the soldiers, and cut off his ear. Jesus said to Peter, "Put up your sword." Then he healed the soldier's ear. Peter drifted into the shadows with the other frightened disciples.

The soldiers bound their prisoner and started for the assembly room where Jesus' enemies were waiting. Peter followed far behind, wondering what he should do and fearing that the soldiers might take him prisoner too.

The soldiers brought Jesus to the house of Annas, and here the trial began.

As Peter stood in the courtyard, a young girl said, "Are you not also one of his disciples?"

Peter was afraid and said, "No, I do not know the man." Peter went to the fire to warm himself. Around the fire stood other men, the high priest's servants and some soldiers. One turned to Peter and asked, "Are you not one of this man's disciples?" Again fear filled Peter's heart, and he replied, "No, I am not!"

A soldier standing by who had seen Peter use his sword said, "I saw you in the garden with him!" Peter cursed and said, "I know not the man!"

Meanwhile the high priest and others had been questioning Jesus and treating him shamefully. They led Jesus away. As he passed by he looked sadly at Peter. Now Peter remembered Jesus' words, "Before the cock crows, you will deny me three times." Peter turned blindly away from the fire, rushed out, and wept bitterly.

Stepping forward, Judas
says, "Hail, Master!"

The Darkest Day in All the World

Matthew 27:1-54; Mark 15:1-39; Luke 23:1-47; John 18:28–19:30

As the trial went on, Judas became greatly troubled. He had hoped that Jesus would free himself from his enemies by some miracle; but Jesus was allowing himself to be helpless in their hands. Judas hurried to the chief priests and scribes, saying, "I have sold an innocent man! I have sinned!"

They looked at him scornfully and asked, "What is that to us? You yourself must answer for your sin." Turning away they refused to take back the money they had given him for betraying Jesus. Judas threw it on the floor of the temple and ran out. Finding a lonely place, he hanged himself.

Soldiers led Jesus before the Roman governor, Pilate, who knew nothing about Jesus. Pilate took him into the judgment hall and talked with him. Afterwards he said, "I find no fault in this man." But the leaders stirred up the mob to shout, "Crucify him! crucify him! He stirs up the people throughout the country, even from Galilee."

When Pilate heard this, he said, "This man belongs to the country that Herod rules." Herod was a son of the king who had tried to kill Jesus when he was a baby. Pilate sent Jesus to Herod at once.

When the soldiers brought Jesus bound with chains, Herod was glad. He hoped that Jesus would do a miracle before him, but Jesus would not answer even one of Herod's questions. With his soldiers Herod mocked Jesus, dressing him in rich robes, and pretending to honor him as a king. Then he sent Jesus back to Pilate.

Now Pilate's wife was greatly troubled about Jesus, for that night she had dreamed about him. She pleaded with her husband to set Jesus free, saying, "He is a just man, not worthy of death."

Pilate, too, wanted to free Jesus. He told the mob, "Both Herod and I have examined this man and find no fault in him."

But the mob cried, "If you set this man free you are no friend of Caesar, and Caesar will not want you for our governor."

Pilate was afraid. He talked to the restless mob about another prisoner, a robber named Barab'bas who had caused the Jews much trouble. Pilate asked, "Shall I release to you Barabbas, the wicked robber, or Jesus?"

With loud cries the mob answered, "Set Barabbas free!"

Pilate asked, "What shall I do with Jesus?" and they answered, "Crucify him! crucify him!"

Taking a basin of water, Pilate washed his hands before the Jews, saying, "I am not guilty of the death of this innocent man."

The Jews cried out, "We ourselves will bear the blame. Let his blood be on our heads!"

Because Pilate wanted to please the people, he called Roman soldiers and told them to lead Jesus away to be crucified. So the trial came to an end.

The Roman soldiers took Jesus and put a crown of thorns upon his head. They put a reed in his hand and bowed before him, saying, "Hail, King of the Jews!" They blindfolded him, spat upon him, and hit him, saying, "Tell us who struck you!" Jesus said not a word. Finally the soldiers took off the purple robe, dressed him in his own clothes, and led him away to be crucified. They gave Jesus and the two robbers heavy crosses to carry.

A crowd of curious people followed the soldiers to the crucifixion. Many in the crowd were Jesus' enemies, others were friends who longed to help but could not. As they went, Jesus fell beneath his heavy cross. The soldiers called a stranger from the crowd to carry the cross.

On the hillside of Calvary the crowd stopped. Soldiers removed the prisoners' clothing and fastened their hands and feet to the crosses. Then they raised the crosses high in the air and planted them firmly in the ground, leaving the prisoners to hang there until they died.

From the cross Jesus prayed, "Father, forgive them, for they know not what they do."

A sign above Jesus' head bore the words, "This is Jesus, the King of the Jews."

One of the thieves who was crucified with Jesus made fun of him. The other said, "We deserve to die, but this man has done no wrong." To Jesus he said, "Lord, remember me when you come into your kingdom."

119

Jesus answered, "Today you shall be with me in paradise."

Sorrowing friends were standing at the foot of Jesus' cross. Among them were his mother and John. Jesus asked John to care for Mary.

Jesus' enemies also stood around the cross. Some of them said, "If you are the King of the Jews, save yourself."

About noon the sky suddenly grew dark. For three hours the great darkness lasted. Then Jesus cried with a loud voice, saying, "It is finished!"

The Roman captain standing near the cross said to his soldiers, "Truly this man was the Son of God."

The Watchers at the Tomb

Matthew 27:55-66; Mark 15:42-47; Luke 23:50-56; John 19:31-42

After the crucifixion a rich man named Joseph came boldly to Pilate and asked to take the body of Jesus and bury it. Joseph loved Jesus. With Pilate's permission Joseph and Nicode'mus went to Calvary, took Jesus' body down from the cross, and wrapped it in fine linen with the sweet spices and perfumes that Nicodemus had brought. Then they laid it in a new grave that Joseph had bought for himself. The grave was cut out of a large rock and opened into a garden.

Jesus' enemies were afraid that his grave might be disturbed by his friends. Hurrying to Pilate they said, "Sir, we remember that Jesus said, 'After three days I will rise again.' Order the grave made sure until the third day, lest his disciples come at night, steal him away, and say to the people, 'He is risen from the dead.'"

Pilate answered, "You have a guard. Go and make the grave as secure as you can."

They went and made the grave sure by sealing the stone and setting a guard.

The women who had watched Joseph and Nicodemus lay Jesus' body away longed to show their love for him. After sunset the next day, when the Sabbath was ended, the women prepared sweet perfumes and planned to go early in the morning to anoint the body of Jesus.

121

Jesus falls beneath the
heavy cross.

But the eleven sorrowing disciples hid themselves. They had forgotten that Jesus had said he would rise again on the third day. Nothing seemed left for them now.

Jesus Rises from the Dead

Matthew 28:1-15; Mark 16:1-11; Luke 24:1-12; John 20:1-18

The hours dragged slowly for the Roman soldiers who guarded Jesus' grave. No one had come. Perhaps they laughed at the Jews for being afraid.

As dawn came the ground began to tremble. Another earthquake had come. The frightened soldiers saw a mighty angel come down, roll the stone from the grave and sit on it. The angel's face was like lightning, and his garments were as white as snow. The soldiers fell to the ground, trembling and helpless, and lay there as if they were dead. As soon as they were able they fled into the city to report to Jesus' enemies.

When the women came to the garden, they found the grave empty. At first they did not see the angel, and they wondered who had stolen the body of their Lord. Mary Mag'dalene ran to tell Peter and John that Jesus' body had been taken away.

After Mary had gone, the other women saw an angel in the tomb. They were afraid and bowed themselves to the ground.

The angel said, "Do not be afraid. Why are you seeking the living among the dead? Jesus is not here; he is risen as he said. Go quickly and tell his disciples and Peter that he is alive and will meet them in Galilee."

The women ran from the place, filled with joy, yet trembling with excitement and fear. The good news seemed too wonderful to be true. Still, they believed and hurried to tell the disciples and other friends.

The disciples could not believe the glad message. Peter and John ran to see for themselves. When they came to the tomb, they found no one, but they saw the graveclothes that Joseph had wrapped around Jesus' body. Peter and John were sure now that Jesus was alive once more.

122

Mary Magdalene had not stayed in the garden long enough to hear the angel's message. Now she returned, longing to find where her Lord had been taken. Entering the garden again, she stood by the empty grave and wept. Then she stooped down, looked into the grave, and saw two angels. One was sitting at the head and another at the foot where Jesus' body had been.

They said to her, "Woman, why are you weeping?"

She replied, "Because they have taken away my Lord and I do not know where they have laid him." Then turning around she saw Jesus himself standing near. But tears blinded her eyes, and she did not know him.

He, too, asked, "Why do you weep?"

Supposing him to be the gardener, she said, "Sir, if you have carried away my Lord, tell me where you have laid him."

Then Jesus said, "Mary!" and she knew his voice. What glad joy filled Mary's heart! She fell at his feet and cried, "Master!"

Jesus said, "Go at once and tell my friends that I will ascend to my Father and your Father, to my God and your God."

While these things were happening, the soldiers were telling the chief priests what had taken place in the garden. The chief priests were greatly alarmed. They quickly called Jesus' other enemies, and all wondered what to do. They offered the soldiers much money if they would promise to tell no one that Jesus had risen or that an angel had opened the tomb.

The Roman soldiers cared nothing about the Jews and their religion. They gladly took the money and went away. And when they were questioned about the disappearance of Jesus' body, they said the disciples stole it while they slept.

The Stranger on the Road to Emmaus

Luke 24:13-35

The Passover Feast over, visitors at Jerusalem were returning home. Along the road leading to Emma'us, a village seven miles from Jerusalem, two men walked slowly, with bowed heads. As they talked about Jesus' trial and crucifixion and about the women's message

that morning, a stranger joined them. He asked, "What are you talking about so earnestly? Why are you sad?"

Cle'opas asked, "Don't you know what has been happening?"

"What things?" the stranger wanted to know.

They answered, "Concerning Jesus of Nazareth, a great prophet in word and deed before God and all the people. The chief priests and rulers condemned him to death and crucified him. We believed he was the Christ.

"This is the third day since it happened and this morning some women of our company astonished us. They had gone early to the tomb, but they did not find Jesus' body. But they saw angels who said, 'He is risen.' Some of us hurried to the grave and found it empty, but we did not see the angels or our risen Lord."

The stranger talked to them about the Christ. He showed them by the Scriptures that Christ would have to suffer these very things and rise again the third day if he would really be the Savior.

When they came to Emmaus, the two said, "Stay with us, for it is almost evening." So the stranger went with them. When they sat down to eat he took bread, blessed it, and gave it to them. At once they knew he was Jesus, the risen Lord. Then he disappeared. How happy they were! Back to Jerusalem they hurried to tell the disciples they had seen the Lord.

Doubting Thomas

Luke 24:36-48; John 20:19-31

The two disciples who had met Jesus on the Emma'us road hurried to Jerusalem to tell the other disciples. When they reached the room where the disciples were, they went in and closed the door. As the two told how Jesus had walked and talked with them, Jesus appeared in their midst.

"Peace be unto you," he said.

But the disciples did not feel peace and quiet in their hearts. They were frightened. Was this a spirit?

To them Jesus said, "Why are you so troubled? Why do you have such thoughts in your hearts? Look at my hands and my feet, and

125

"Why are you sad?" the Stranger asks
two men on the road to Emmaus.

you will see that it is I. Touch me and you will know that I am not a spirit. A spirit does not have flesh and bones.

The disciples looked at his hands and feet. It really was the Lord. They were so amazed that they didn't know what to do.

"Have you anything here to eat?" Jesus asked. And they gave him broiled fish and honey.

Then Jesus opened their understanding of the Scriptures. He said, "Christ had to suffer and to rise from the dead the third day. Now repentance and remission of sins must be preached to all nations, beginning at Jerusalem. You are witnesses of these things."

How the disciples rejoiced at their visit with Jesus! Thomas had not been with the disciples when Jesus came. Joyfully they told him, "We have seen the Lord."

But Thomas answered, "Unless I place my finger in the print of the nails in his hands and place my hand on his side, I will not believe."

Eight days passed. Again the disciples were together in a room, and the doors were shut. This time Thomas was with him. As suddenly as before, Jesus appeared to them and said, "Peace be to you!"

While the disciples marveled at Jesus' strange coming, he spoke to Thomas, "Put your finger in my hands and place your hand on my side. Do not doubt but believe."

Falling to his knees Thomas said, "My Lord and my God!"

Jesus told Thomas, "Because you have seen me, you believe. Blessed are those who believe even though they have not seen me."

Jesus' Last Meeting with His Disciples

Mark 16:15-19; Luke 24:50-53; Acts 1:1-14

For forty days after Jesus rose from the dead, he often talked with his disciples about the kingdom of God. Each time they saw him they worshiped him. Still they did not understand that his kingdom would not be an earthly one.

At their farewell meeting, Jesus said, "All power is given unto me in heaven and in earth. Go ye therefore, and teach all nations, baptizing them in the name of the Father, and of the Son, and of the Holy Ghost."

As they talked together, Jesus said, "John the Baptist baptized you with water, but you shall be baptized with the Holy Spirit in a few days. You shall receive power from heaven when the Holy Spirit comes upon you. You will witness boldly of me in Jerusalem, in Judea, in Samaria, and in the farthest parts of the world. But do not go away from Jerusalem until the Holy Spirit is given you."

When he had said this, Jesus was lifted up into heaven. The disciples watched until he disappeared. As they stood looking upward, two angels clothed in white came to them. The angels said, "Men of Galilee, why do you stand looking into heaven? This same Jesus who is taken up into heaven will come again in the same way as he went away."

The disciples returned to Jerusalem. In the upper room they met with other friends of Jesus to wait and pray until the Holy Spirit should be given them. No longer were they sad. Great joy filled their hearts. They knew that Jesus was really the Christ, the Savior, the Son of God.

D